The Supreme Future

BY
THE SPIRIT OF THE FATHER GOD
THROUGH HIS SERVANT
HRM KING SOLOMON DAVID JESSE ETE
(King Solomon Spiritual Library)
Eteroyal Universal Family

HIS ROYAL MAJESTY
KING SOLOMON DAVID JESSE
ETE
The Senior Christ Servant

BROTHERHOOD OF THE CROSS AND STAR

All rights reserved
Copyright © Solomon ETE, 2008
Solomon ETE is hereby identified as author
of this work in accordance with Section 77
of the Copyright,
Designs and Patents Act 1988

The book cover picture is copyright
to Solomon ETE
King Solomon Spiritual Library
P O BOX 27394
London E12 6WW UK
www.kingsolomonspirituallibrary.com

This book is published by Lulu

This book is sold subject to the conditions that it shall not, by way of trade or otherwise, be lent, resold, hired out or otherwise circulated without the author's or publisher's prior consent in any form of binding or cover other than that in which it is published and without a similar condition including this condition being imposed on the subsequent purchaser.

A CIP record for this book is available from
the British Library
ISBN 978-0-9559801-0-7

Content

CONTENT	PAGES
INTRODUCTION	11-16
SHARING	16-28

A: APPROVED ARTICLE OF SHARING

B: NONE APPROVED ARTICLE OF SHARING

HEART	28-39

A: COMMUNICATION

B: APPROVED COMMUNICATION

C: NONE APPROVED COMMUNICATION

MIND	39-49

A: CONTROLLING OF THE MIND

B: LOOSE MIND

FORMATION OF A GOOD TEMPLATE   49-75

A: GOOD ROOT

B: UPROOTING A BAD ROOT

HUMAN BEHAVIOUR
76-94

A: PERMANENT BEHAVIOUR

B: UNAPPROVED CHARACTER

C: APPROVED CHARACTER

SOULS   94-109

A: FORMATION OF SOULS INTO THE POSITIVE PARADISE OF GOD

B: DESTRUCTION OF SOULS INTO THE HELL OF SATAN

PEACEFUL NEW WORLD
110-116

A: SUPREME FAITH WITH THE HOLY FATHER

B: seventy-two million characters

MANIFESTATION OF GOD, THE SERVANTS GLORY
117-131

A: THROUGH THE NAME AND THE BLOOD OF OUR LORD JESUS CHRIST

B: ALL GLORY BELONGS TO THE FATHER GOD THE CREATOR OF THE UNIVERSE

C: THROUGH THE OFFICE OF EMPOWERMENT, LEADER OLUMBA OLUMBA OBU

DENOMINATIONS
131-133

A: CHURCHES

B: OTHER ORGANIZATIONS

C: CHRISTIANITY

D: MUSLIM

E: JUDAISM

F: HINDUS

G: Buddhism

H: OTHERS

HUMAN MEAT   134-139

A: FOOD AND DRINK

B: VEGETARIANISM

COVER YOUR NAKEDNESS   140-146

A: PHYSICAL DRESS

B: SPIRITUAL DRESS

C: MIND AND SPIRIT

GREETINGS   147-149

A: SOCIAL GREETING

B: SPIRITUAL GREETING

INTERACTIONS   149-162

A: MINDFUL INTERACTION

B: CAREFULNESS

C: GENERAL CARE

THE FUTURE 163-214

A: ARRANGEMENT

B: DIVINE LIFE

C: MANIFESTATION OF WORLD PEACE

D: LIVE AND LET LIVE

E: MIND YOUR BUSINESS

F: MARRIAGE, NEW OFFSPRING

G: CONTINUITY

H: ONE WORLD IDEOLOGY

I: UNIVERSAL GODS

AO: SOCIAL AMENITIES

AA: THE TRUE SERVANTS

AB: EVERYTHING IS FATHER, FATHER, FATHER

CONCLUSION 215-226

A: DIVINE NATURE OF HUMAN BEINGS ON EARTH

B: NOT ONLY IN THIS GLORY BUT IN ALL PLANET OF MANIFESTATION EXIST THE FOLLOWING CHARACTERS;

C: HUMAN FATHERS

D: FATHER AND MOTHER

E: CHILDREN

F: RELATIVES

G: RELATIONS

H: FRIENDSHIPS WITH GOD

I: WITH FATHER AND MOTHER

AO: WITH BROTHERS AND SISTER

AA: AND ALL POSITIVE HUMAN BEING IN GENERAL

THE SPIRITUAL BUDGET   227-273

ABC OF WORD   274-284

WITH LOVE   285

KING SOLOMON SPIRITUAL LIBRARY

THE GOD ENCYCLOPAEDIA

WORD OF INFINITY

FATHER'S TALK

(GOD PRESENT)

Christ our Lord, First Bartholomew,
Father Two Thousand and Seven
(OA.OI.BOOG)
(Saturday, First September, Year Two
Thousand and Seven (01.09.2007))

In The Name Of Our Lord Jesus Christ In The Blood Of Our Lord Jesus Christ Now And Forever More Amen!

Today is the sixth day of the celebration of the New Covenant of God on earth, for this year. It pleases **ME, THE FATHER GOD THE CREATOR OF THE UNIVERSE, THE DIVINE AND SUPREME WORD**, to manifest this wonderful Lecture Revelation called, **THE SUPREME FUTURE.**

INTRODUCTION

I brought this Lecture Revelation out from The Spiritual Library of **THE FATHER GOD** so that the entire universe will know **MY** mind and what **I** have in place for the future. The future is **THE FATHER GOD HIMSELF. I, THE SUPREME FATHER, I AM THE FUTURE**. I exist as the **EXISTENCE** and have never gone backwards and never will. **I AM** always future every second, every minute, every hour, every day, every week, every month, every year and forever. **I AM The Future**.
I AM THE SUPREME FUTURE. I decoded this information called **The Supreme Future** today, which mean this title of word, none, has ever heard

until now. **The Supreme Future** is the last hope and the last destination for every soul in all the planets terrestrials and celestial and all the rest of them.
ALL PLANETS OF MANIFEST TAKE HEED AND NOTE THAT THIS IS THE LAST BUS STOP FOR EVERY CREATION. **I** took **MY** time to bring out this information and register it as posterity on earth so that all earth dwellers from now till eternity will use this in all their individual human undertakings.
THE SUPREME FUTURE is the companion for all human beings.
Whenever any human being comes into this world from the nature of any of the four living creatures namely, either **man,** as Human-God, **animal** as human-animal, **bird** as human-bird or **fish**

as human-fish, including organisms that improved to become humans, **THE SUPREME FUTURE** is the manual of modus operandi. The only office for any nature to progress is when they manifest and come into the physical world for improvement.

Use this information to wish yourself good-luck and to wish yourself anything good. If you need any spiritual power or any backup to have the Supreme Energy around you for maximum protection, maximum insurance, maximum coverage, and maximum security in all its forms, this is your companion to assist you achieve them. It is not a secret society thing. It is not initiation idea.

This is from **THE SUPREME FATHER GOD ALMIGHTY** and this is **THE SUPREME FUTURE,** motivated by **THE UNIVERSAL SUPREME WORD ALMIGHTY "THE MOTIVATOR OF LIFE"**. **I** have now activated **The Supreme Future** and have attached **MY** energy from today, because of the new covenant **I** had with mankind that - After Those Days says The Lord, The Most High, **I** will come and live in human again as **I** lived before in man and manifest **MY** glory through man so that mankind will have peace. As the heavenly bodies have peace so everybody on earth must have peace. Peace shall reign everywhere. This constitutes **THE SUPREME FUTURE.**

Any authority that will try in any way, manner or form to fight against this authority will be arrested and will become wanted soul in spirit, soul and physical truth. Any government, any denomination, any authority of any form, angel or spirit that kick against this **SUPREME FUTURE,** the word from **THE HOLY FATHER GOD ALMIGHTY** will have themselves, himself or herself to blame.

I AM therefore, urging the whole universe, all nations small and big, humans and spirits to adopt the new **SUPREME FUTURE SYSTEM** to their lives. It will change bad environment to good one. This is the introductory part of this Lecture Revelation Supreme Information called **THE SUPREME FUTURE, THE DIVINE REVELATION FROM THE DIVINE FATHER GOD.**

This word came out from the mind of love, the computerised mind of God, the Comprehensive and Ability unlimited Memory of **THE FATHER GOD** to human kind, including all creations because **I AM THE SUPREME FUTURE.**

SHARING

A: APPROVED ARTICLE OF SHARING

The first thing in the future is sharing. What do you share? **I, THE FATHER THE CREATOR OF THE UNIVERSE** is love. The Spirit of love brings sharing. What do you share? What are the things you share with one another? **THE FATHER GOD** is the author of everything. **HE** is the owner of everything. **HE** is life. Therefore, anything you share in this world with one another must be based on love. No human being is authorized to formulate any idea that is negative, for instance incantations, secret societies and such negative evil things.

No one is authorized to bring such to share with anybody. If you should do that you are causing problems to your soul. You are emphatically banned from doing that. You are not authorized to share any negativism with anybody from this day. You are not authorized to share any rubbish and any idea that is not positive, with anybody. You are

not permitted to share a practice that is not positive and you must not share any conduct that is not positive. You are not authorized to share any word or share any information, anything at all that is not positive with anyone.
Anything that is negative which will pollute the world or destroy it as well as destroy mankind, you are not permitted to share it. Any form of sharing that destroys humankind; any form of idea that destroys man – any idea that is negative, vile and evil you do not and need not and must not share with anyone. Whether you are a president, head of state or governor, King or Queen do not share any evil with any one. Whatever and whoever you are god; spirit or angel and wherever you come from you must not share

any negative and evil information or ideas with anybody.

What you now share with people is the word of God, the word of life, humility, peace, harmony, joy, patience and all other attributes of **THE FATHER GOD ALMIGHTY.** Anything that is positive that allows mankind's life to be comfortable you can share with people.

Since **I THE FATHER GOD, I AM** love, **I** talk about good life. Share with one another anything that is positive, anything that is good. Reciprocate goodness and good things amongst yourselves and between one another. If you share what is good with people you will continue to improve. Any article or anything that is positive you share with one another, but anything that destroys life like smoking, drinking, fornication and adultery – anything at all you do that affects humans adversely, you do not share such ideas. You must not share the practice and must not interact with people in such negative manner or communicate such ideas because that is not what the sharing is about. The sharing is on what **THE FATHER GOD ALMIGHTY** approves.

As **I** said, the act of sharing is on things and activities **THE FATHER GOD** recommends, because they will bring peace. Share good ideas and other good practices like love, peace, and humility. Teach people to practice these good virtues and exude them. If you carry the positive training and the positive ideas from The School of Higherself and educate people and also, if you impact this information to human kind, then you are sharing with **THE FATHER'S** mind. You are indeed sharing with **THE FATHER GOD'S** good spirit and you will be elevated. If you share good ideas, good information, The Father's Talk, Higherself training and all the good things that you know from the freewill of mind, that such things are positive and will help one another, then **I** will promote you, very, very high. Conversely, any negativism you practice and share with other people, that will result in you being reduced to nothingness. **I** will so reduce you to be low, low, and real low and lower until you no longer exist in spirit, soul, physical and otherwise.

B: **NON-APPROVED ARTICLE OF SHARING**

I have already mentioned unapproved articles of sharing

above. You do not need to drink intoxicating drinks and you must not offer such drinks to people. You must not smoke or sniff any substances and you must not offer them to people. Anything that has bad effect and influence on people you must not offer to people and must not take or have them. Why are intoxicating drinks, drugs, smoking and so on, not well and good? Such substances fuel excitement, are intoxicating, and clouds reasoning, which in many cases result in misbehaviour. The negative spirit uses them to control people. So, avoid intoxicating drinks, do not take hard drugs, smoke or sniff substances and do not offer them to anyone. Do not perpetrate such act of wickedness on anybody. Some men give women intoxicating drinks or slip some substances in their drinks to take advantage of the women and do whatever they liked to them. You are destroying your soul with that behaviour. You therefore, must stop that attitude to save your soul. If indeed you give people drinks to get them drunk so that you can control them, you are evil and **THE FATHER'S** angels will deal with you. This is the kind of destruction that people bring on to visit them-selves, not God destroying you. You will use your hands to destroy yourself.

Therefore, materials and activities that not approved are you must not smoke, sniff or take substances. You must not drink anything or take any drugs that changed your normal character to rubbish. You must not practice negativism at all and must not do anything bad to

change people from the original character God gave them. Injecting substances into people, drinks, food, medications and also using human blood and human gene to practice negativism in order to turn human beings into behaving the way you want so that you control them, those are acts of wickedness. Anybody that goes out of his or her way to control another human being fights against God. You want to make yourself equal with **THE FATHER GOD;** you will be arrested and put in Hell. *This is not a joke. It is exactly what will happen.*
You will remind yourself of this when you see things happening around you, you are not happy with. You will feel and see the differences in your life at each turn of untoward happenstance

and you will be arrested. You will certainly feel it when you are arrested, by which you should know that your attitude and your practices are not approved. All these things will happen spiritually. **I** have not sent any human being on this earth to arrest anybody or put anybody in prison for nothing went you do not know the kind of truly offensive the person committed. **I** have angels that will do the job more than you human, but all criminal offenders must be punish. So leave people alone. Everybody should practice live and let live, and as a good citizen of the world, you must respect and obey a good and positive government of the land, which are directly represent God, from today and from now on and for eternity. **THE FATHER GOD** has armies, angels and soldiers that know what is good and they will do it spiritually also. No human being is authorised to arrest anybody or torment anybody or act in any way to people or somebody that portrays you are controlling him or her for no good reasons. **THE FATHER GOD** will control the whole world with all **HIS** angels.

Things unapproved includes any idea which you know is negative and you extend such to people; being a member of secret societies like the occult, engaging in occultism and other evil practices, burning of incense, burning of candles to invoke evil spirit, invocations - calling on ghosts, angels and other demonic spirits, getting involved in all sorts of things to commit wicked acts, perpetrating evil negative vile acts. These things are not permitted. These attitudes are diabolical and taboo and as such not permitted in the services and the premises of THE FATHER GOD which is the whole universe in all circumstances of life. Anybody therefore, involved in these unapproved acts will suffer the consequences of their actions. That is what **I THE FATHER GOD** decided to reveal today so that the whole world will know that **THE FATHER GOD** does not approve anything negative.

A thought could occur to you to make money or to enter into a relationship with somebody. Anything that you do, any motive or intentions that when you execute such you gain something from somebody and you know that to get the result you want, you have to be involved in negative evil activity, stop, do not do it! If you went ahead and involved yourself, you have destroyed your soul. Not just your soul, you will have also destroyed your physical self and your offspring, because your birth back into the earth plane will not augur well.

HEART

A: COMMUNICATION

The heart of human self is where everything emanates from. Everything you think of in this world came from the heart, **THE SUPREME WORD OF THE UNIVERSE** – everything and anything at all! The heart is the spiritual home for all spirits. You can envisage a human being, but what you cannot see is the heart – the human heart. In the human heart lies memory and from that memory emerges the power of communication.

There are approved communications and unapproved communications. Man is not authorized to speak negative words, because it is from the thought that all the evil happens in the whole world. What is approved for mankind is to communicate in a positive manner. Speak what is good. Make good pronouncements. Man is not allowed to curse.

You must not curse anyone neither formulate any evil thing nor communicate any evil ideas through any form be it mass communication, any written manner, pronouncements of any sort or verbal discussions of any kind. You must not think evil. If any evil thought comes to you, make the pronouncement, '**GOD**

FORBID BAD THING!' If you have read the Lecture Revelation called **'Button Of Hold'** you would know the rest of it. Nonetheless, say it as **I AM** saying it here now, make the pronouncement '***God forbid bad thing!***' Say the words even if you do not believe in God because some people are funny and say they do not believe in God, and that there is nothing like God. The meaning of God is Good Nature - Nature Father and Nature Mother – Supreme Nature and that is **THE SUPREME FUTURE.** This name God is coined from Good, through Acts of Good Intentions. Satan is acts of bad intentions. If you do not believe that there is something called God, but you believe that there is a good thing, a good mind, a good idea, comfortable life and positive things, then you are a believer. God means positive things and good means all positives like good treatments, good thoughts, good acts and good everything. If therefore, you believe in good treatments, love and everything good and nice, then you believe in God. Believing in the good things ensue the approved communications from you that **I THE FATHER GOD, I AM GOOD.** Think well, speak well and hear well so that it will manifest event that is well and form a good atmosphere for everybody on earth to rejoice. War is very devastating to the parties involved, particularly individuals in the heart of it. War spoils the atmosphere of a country and makes people panic and run helter-skelter. Children suffer including the old and everybody else. Consequently, those who cause wars are forever in punishment, because you put people through terrifying ordeal. You subject people to great sufferings and lamentation. They suffer loss of property, lives and everything else. Therefore, untold punishments await those who use politics and pomposity in all their forms as well as pride and arrogance to think up nonsense and in so doing cause war that affect human lives so badly. If a human being is satisfied in the position that God gave him or her, they will not plan war and certainly not plan a coup to oust another person. These are amongst the types of unapproved communications and actions.

You should not publish magazines, books or for that matter any publications at all that displays indecent human anatomies or naked flesh and you call them models. These things are not permitted in the New World of **SUPREME FUTURE**. No human being should be seen naked in any form. Or, then indeed you are mad, non compos mentis and therefore demonstrating your insanity with nudity. All the girls, boys, women and men that go naked in the form of profession called mode, playboys and playgirls for instance, in their next incarnation they will go mad and walk about naked. It will be that the spirit of madness came into you, because you took voluntary evolution for yourself in your previous physical manifest, which is what you are doing now as you are going about naked and involved in obscene behaviours. Or nature would take it upon itself to make you madness and also as an animal that have no clothing, no idea and no sense - nothing. You will go back to being animal, because you come from animal and still reveal yourself on earth that you are an animal. In the animal kingdom they do not wear cloth.

B: APPROVED COMMUNICATION

I created man differently. Man covers their nakedness as a mark of superiority amongst all other creations on earth. When somebody says they are models and whose work involves indecent flesh exposure, it means they are beasts. It goes for all that behave in like manner. You display your breasts, bottom and or expose all of you. Therefore, you are an animal. That is one of the things that shows you are a human-animal. That is how animals behave. These groups of people cannot be classified amongst the category of mankind the Human-Gods. They have no dignity. They are not respectful Human as the Image GOD. In your form, if you have money or you are rich, the money helps you display more of the animal you are. Money is manmade and when you die you come back to be a dog or any such animal in nature.

Those who sleep with dogs including other animals and fornicate with them and do all sorts of abominable things with them are beasts. These types of bad communications portray you to be animals and **I** do not permit animal's evil instincts in the Kingdom of human God nature. Mind you that the whole universe and all the planets are now Kingdom of God and Jehovah God and His Christ are ruling them with His divine angels. So, if you practice any of these things and communicate in these manners you voluntarily take evolution to be human-animal and you are going to be in Hell – amongst the mad people. Therefore, communications that are approved include sending peace to everybody, think well, speak and talk well, see well, hear well and do well. All articles, all publications should be positive. There should be positive news in the air. All television channels, radios, Internets – all forms of media should publish good news. You should for instance, announce how people gave birth and all went well; how people married and it went well, and are going well and how people sleep well, and wake up well. You should give positive news, which would encourage people to do positive things, not all the time you are reported evils and negatives news.

C: **NON-APPROVED COMMUNICATION**

What obtains in the world now is that bad news get all the attention and so when people want to be in the news, they do evil things and sure enough the news media flag their actions and disseminate this negative news to all and sundry. As news coverage in the world is on evil and negative and horrific things, evil spirit trying to controls the world and the practice of evil abound, because directly or indirectly you are promoting negativism. That has to stop, now!

THE FATHER GOD has come to take over and to take charge of administrations of the whole universe in the spiritual and in the physical presence, so the evil news will cease to exist. The evil people and the carnal ones do not get excited when they hear positive news. They are more excited with news of death, disaster and all sorts of upheaval, and that at the moment in this world makes money. The negative energy for that reason continued to causes problems to create news. This must stop.

From the time you no longer promote evil news; you do not promote negative scenes; you desist from promoting negative communication evil will cease. When all the negative communications, all the negative write-ups and negative readings and negative teachings as well as all the negative magazines and everything negative cease in the world, including all the evil communications and evil plans, evils in all its multiform and all sorts of unapproved things that are practiced in this world ceased, good environments flourishes. When all these things cease, then you will see that the world is a pleasant place to live. That is of the utmost importance to the future living here in this world so says **THE FATHER GOD THE CREATOR OF THE UNIVERSE** this day; the above is only remedies for all natural disaster that awaited mankind because of man disobedient to the voice of **THE FATHER GOD**.

MIND

A: **CONTROLLING OF MIND**

Heart then Mind: The Lecture Revelation titled 'After Heart and After Mind' dealt more on this. Mind is the home of carnal self. In the human endeavour, human character and the human life, **I** made the mind to be the harbour of all the technologies. All improvements, science and scientific things are from the mind while the heart is the spiritual home for **THE FATHER GOD**. The heart must give approval on everything the mind presents. When the mind generates an idea, it leaves it for the heart for proper refinement and this takes effect in the Thinking and Reasoning faculties in brain. In-depth writing on this in the book titled 'HE IS THE WORD'. Read it if you want to know more on Thinking and Reasoning faculties.

The mind has to be controlled by the positive thoughts, which come from your heart – your real heart-real self and not what you copied from somebody else. Those who *follow-follow* (follow sheepishly or easily led) are not controlled by their heart rather they are controlled by their mind. In human creation the female's nature represents the mind. That is the reason it is easy to manipulate women. It is easy to manipulate women in the negative ways. However, now in the Advanced Spirit of God which is Christ including the Positive part of **THE FATHER GOD,** as well as the Wisdom, the Knowledge and the office of Understanding, there is no woman and there is no man. Therefore, do not allow your mind to control you anymore. You should rather control your mind,

because everything that is controlled by the lower mind brings problems. The lower mind has been bringing problems on earth. Everybody must from henceforth listen to his or her heart. ***Think well, speak well, hear well and do well.***
When somebody brings an idea to you, give it a good thought and go over it properly. Allow your innerself to absorb the idea before you accept, and also think of the end result of your acceptance. You should control your mind with positive thoughts, and positive attitudes and not negative vibes, because if you allow the negative to control your mind it is likely to lead you to do something you should not do. That would then bring evil communication that could result in anger. When you are annoyed you could say

unnecessary things, and then pride comes, which would not let you back down on your opinion whether good or bad. Greed could also ensue from the evil communication that could result in war. You will then start to cease other country's property. With greed you go to the bank to steal money. Greediness leads to all sorts of bad behaviour, other bad and evil things. All the evils are generated from your mind because it controls you. At the end of the day you suffer the consequences of your evil actions. On the contrary, you stand to benefit with a positive mind. The positive heart will bring to you the positive mind.

Generating good thoughts in your heart will approve the exact positive things you have in your mind. That is the future conduct, future thinking, future behaviour and future practice of the positive minds.

The minds of the positive people always bring good things. Those who promote the world with all the positive technologies are the positive minds. They bring good things to improve human lives. They have positive ideologies and everybody should work on improving themselves on positive things.

B: **LOOSE MIND**

Loose mind is when somebody cannot control his or her mind. You are *follow-follow* (follow sheepishly or easily led) person. Pretentiousness and *follow-follow* abound outrageously on earth in entire world. As a matter of fact ninety-nine percent of the people on earth follow things blindly and sheepishly. People join the occult without reasoning properly what they are getting into.

You see somebody drive a nice car and you are not aware that the spirit of evil, the master of occultism bought that car for that person. This person apparently has been instructed to drive around and attract attention and that anyone who wants to be as rich as you are, bring such persons to come and join us, so that they too would start to donate blood. That is how people get trapped into evil practices, because their mind is loose and therefore cannot stand firm in their positive way.

A real gentleman, a real person in the positive nature does not *follow-follow*. These types of persons are not easily led and so hardly misled. They will know exactly the type of person you are

before they get involved with you. So from today as you have had access to this companion, do not allow yourself to be misled. Always think well.
Observe the type of communication. Observe the type of things that come into your mind. Also observe the type of information you have. From there you will know exactly what to do. If you keep to this principle you will not *follow-follow* that is you cannot follow someone blindly or easily misled. If you do not follow blindly you will not have loose mind. Some people loose their minds and consequently miss a lot of things in life, which were supposed to be good in their future. This is because evil and all the evil people gang against you. Everything is two, positive and negative. Assuming there is

somebody who wants to marry you and you do not know this person's future being that at present this person is not yet rich. Your friends would discourage you from the impending marriage and asked you to reconsider on marrying someone without a proper job. 'Are you going to marry this person who is not well educated? Are you going to marry this person that is not this and not that?' They would put these questions across to you. You will now have two frames of mind and also you are not sure of the intentions of your friends. You cannot say for sure whether they genuinely concerned for you or are jealous, as they don't have any husband or wife as the case may be. It could be that if you left the relationship they jump on board with your intended husband or wife. You heeded to these things – pressure or advice with the reason that someone is your friend, your mama, your papa or your relation, but you may not know the real reason behind their dissuading you from going ahead with marrying this person. When you have loose mind you accepted ill advices and could lose your future brightness. Think well by yourself. You the advisers don't go about and spoiling people's mind. Do not trap people into having loose minds for you to easily mislead them and consequently they lose their blessings. Allow everybody to let their hearts direct them so that they can decide what they have in their minds, and approved by their hearts for them. When you leave people alone you will not share with their problems. In contrast, if after advising someone and they have loose mind and miss what would have been good for them, then you will suffer the result, because the same thing will happen to you. What you sow is what you reap. You cannot go back to say oh, sorry I did not know that things would turn so bad for you I would not have given you such advice. Since you gave the advice and it resulted in mistake, two of you will share in the mistake. That is what I mean by saying do not have loose mind. Loose mind is evil. It is loose mind that made Adam to join Eve. Loose mind made Eve accept the instructions from the serpent. Loose mind can lead one to do anything that is not good. It is therefore imperative to be strong in your mind when you make decisions.

FORMATION OF A GOOD TEMPLATE

If you have taken note of this Lecture Revelation so far and had obtained information from most of the other Lectures of **THE FATHER'S TALK (GOD PRESENT)** from The Universal Information Centre, King Solomon Spiritual Library, The School of The Higherself Brotherhood Mastership, you are a Brotherhood. Through this forum you obtain the certificate to grow above your carnal self.

You will grow above misunderstanding.

You grow above pride and arrogance.

You will grow above evil mind and loose mind.

You will grow above all sorts of things that do not bring glory to

God and your good nature as human God.
You are then on the road to establishment.
The road to establishment is the formation of good character, the formation of template from bad to good and from evil to righteousness and holy things and from negative to positive. This took effect because of good conducts. If you yield energy, which is good by thinking good thoughts, speaking well, hear well and doing good acts, and even if you came from the bad side and even if your mama and your papa are bad and you have bad template, then because of your good practice here physically now, you have voluntarily taken evolution to good life now and in your future. **I will then create a new template for you. I AM THE**

SUPREME FUTURE, THE ORIGINAL FUTURE, I will create the new template that in future your offspring will start to be good.

If your papa is a native doctor and or witchcraft and your mama is witchcraft and your husband equally is witchcraft or your wife as the case may be –
If you also found out that in the family they practice incantations and idol worshipping -they are full of pride and arrogance and causing all sorts of problems in the world -
If you discovered that your family are amongst the group that on being made president they go to war – war, war, war all the time -
If you discovered that in your family when they are in position of authority they siphon government money and do all

sorts of evil things and do not think of the welfare of people – On knowing these things you decided and came out of that family. At the moment in your life, you occupy important position in the society and you are well known. Luckily, you are now exposed to this information here in this **Supreme Future Lecture Revelation,** which is directly come from **ME THE FATHER GOD THE CREATOR OF THE UNIVERSE.** This Lecture Revelation has inspired you and you now know and understand things and situations differently. You know that you will suffer the consequences of your actions and so you shun the ways of life of your family you disassociated from. Of utmost importance is the wonderful opportunity to take evolution to a good formula – the formula of **THE SUPREME FUTURE** that will change your environment and entire universe. That will change you and give you new template to form a new offspring.

A template is blood. Anything that you are involved with most of the time is the energy you will yield. If you are involved with an idea, an interest or activity or any form of action say, sports, you will yield that. Your involvement with anything could be spiritual or physical and after seventy-two hours it will start to yield energy in you. That energy is the blood in the physical body, but in spirit it forms the soul of incarnation. In the case of a man, if you get your wife or any woman you are with pregnant within the seventy-two hours you are intensely involved with your idea, interest or activity;

she will give birth to one of the energy you yield. That constitute the offspring you have established. That is the template you have now created on earth and your next birth back into the earth plane will be from your new offspring. You have now established a new template, a new file, and new folder in the record. When you read the Lecture Revelation titled **'Husband, Wife, Child, Office, Cabinet and Record'** you will see this information in details.

The position you see yourself in and what you are doing is part character of your parents and also what you are born with. The template you inherited is by blood, whether you were procreated through fornication, adultery or your papa and mama slept together to beget you. That was when you inherited your template.

How then do you feature the template? You feature the template through what you do on earth. The continuation of your character, your life endeavours, activities and behaviours including everything else, all combine and yield the energy inside you which is your blood. When you then use that energy to bring forth a child, you form a new template. Therefore, to advance a good future requires that you do good things, practice good things and do away with all the negative minds including negative ideas. Rebuke all the bad news you hear and all the bad advices you gathered from friends as well as family.

You must disassociate yourself from evil people and evil groups. People that drink and smoke, people involved in nudity and indecent body exposure and those who live abominable lives you should avoid.

You need to also disassociate your mind and your actions from those who insult their elders, their parents and others as well as all the people that do all sorts of other bad things. What will then replace them are good characters and the five stars namely, mercy, love, righteousness, kindness and peace. These will start to take root in your mind and that is voluntary evolution to a new formula.

I, THE FATHER GOD your **CREATOR** and your Nature, will thereafter, reformat you in the soul and give you a new template that will establish you in the new life. When you go and come back - being that nobody dies - everybody goes and comes back – you will come back through your new template. It is recycling process. Do not say 'when I die I go'. You certainly do not go anyway.

To be a member of **THE SUPREME FUTURE,** the Divine Future, does away with bad things. That is the reason **I** brought this case study so that from now, which is the present, if you do well you correct the past. If you read the Lecture Revelation, '**Past, Present and Future**' you will come across where **I, THE FATHER GOD** provided the opportunity for people to improve. The evolution you take is from the decision you made for yourself. It is from your own mind and from your own belief.

If you believe this Lecture Revelation that it is not ordinary and that it is from **THE FATHER GOD,** and if it makes sense at all to you, you will stand to gain a lot.

Anything that is good, anything that makes sense, anything that has sound idea and that there is something you can benefit from this, do not throw it away. By not throwing this information away and believing in it and adopt all the messages you gathered from **THE FATHER'S TALK,** your life will change for good now and even then, the future.

A: **GOOD ROOT**

When a good template is established at formation, then the good template will give good root. Root is the formula. Root is the template. From the beginning of time **I** call that **Sarantics and Sarantors** – the forefathers, the Root of David.

Why the positive ones on earth are called the Root of David? Abraham is from the Root of

David, but Abraham was on earth before David. Why did our Lord Jesus Christ say '***I am the Morning Star, the Root of David***?' This is because the Root of David out of the entire human race is positive and that is Abel. Abel is the positive Son of **THE FATHER GOD THE CREATOR OF THE UNIVERSE.** In the whole universe, the tribe of Abel, the Root of Abel is the only positive Root. The Root of Cain is the vampires, the witchcrafts and all the people that practice evil, demons and everything negative.

Those who finished their seven incarnations and seven generations from the Root of Cain turn to be demons and animals. **I** revealed how Satan and Demons formed. **I THE FATHER GOD** did not create them per se. They are formed by dirt, which **I** revealed through a demonstration. **I** revealed that if you dug a big hole on the ground and poured in water to get a poodle, and then threw in all the waste, excreta and all the refuse and left it for days. After seventy-two hours, nature would then use the fermented refuse, rubbish, dirt, excreta inside the poodle now called, ***NEARER ENERGY*** to form insects like, mosquitoes, flies, maggots, cockroaches, rats and all sorts of dirty insects and dirty animals. Three months from the seventy-two hours other things would form too from that collection of waste inside that poodle Evil of Satan form in that manner. Those dirty animals are witchcrafts and the vampires. When flies from that resulted stench perched on your food they give you poison. Animals breed in dirty environments and are formed by dirt. These dirty creatures will not form in clean environments. Conclusively, these vile insects and other creatures and some animals are formed by dirt. Witchcraft, elementary spirits, and demons all form in similar manner.

Your bad character, your bad pronouncements, your bad words, your bad practices and the evil things you do form dirt in your system and you do not know this. You are annoyed, you kill, you curse and you plan evil. All negative things you do and all the evil that you practice go into your system.

You go about taking rounds in hotels engaging in prostitution and its other forms – escorts and special escort, *ashawo,* flat girls – all those satanic names. People formulate these things to pollute people and to form death in the atmosphere. What goes on in the midst of them is drunkenness, smoking, using and abusing drugs and all sorts of evil practices. These are the practices of witchcraft, other evil practices, evil communication and all the evil system in the whole world. They form evil templates everywhere.

People fornicate about in the street and in so doing Satan uses such action to form templates. When eventually the energy manifested as a child, the child grew to behave anyhow, because this person already have the spirit of fornication in him or her. The template of prostitution is what you inherited and the template is your blood cells. The life of a prostitute you are living features your template. To change the template you have to start to lead good life. The Lecture Revelation, **'Husband, Wife and Child, Office, Cabinet and File'** enumerated the truth about this. A child you had when you started to do good things will have different character from the ones you had when you were bad. All your children are your energy. They are the souls you formed and must therefore be given birth to. If you do not give birth to them, they stay behind to disturb you. To create a good template is necessary especially for the future. The good template replaces the bad one so that when you are reborn into the world you are not born as evil or mixed template that is, positive and negative because of parasite present in the blood of your parents.

Summarily, when somebody is born on the earth through bad template, for instance fornication, the evil, which is the spirit of prostitution, is inborn. This person would then materialize the negative spirit through their character, ideas and events because the evil is in them already. It is the root. If the person is positive, the Positive Spirit, God will materialize in the same way in the person with good character.

Formation of bad template is a formation root. People like Pharaoh, Nebuchadnezzar, Pilate, Caesar, Hitler and De Lawrence – all the animals that came to this world as human beings created negative things. Spencer for instance, established the

Rosicrucian Order. All of them are human-animals and are Satan's agents. They came to this world through evil templates that were formed. As these people were here on earth physically they have dropped their spirits soul and ideas on earth.

So now if you sleep with the men or women that have links with these evil people, you are providing the means for these souls to manifest again physically in the world. These souls are constantly looking for a way to come back to the world. That is the reason there are lots of evil practices on earth – native doctors, soothsayer, numerous others and all sorts of things.

I revealed about the Seven Angels I refused them crossing over back to Heaven when they came to the earth. They became soothsayers'

spirits and all the oracles. They
dropped their spirits souls about.
Their children are the false
prophets on earth. To rid the world
of these evils change your attitude
of fornication, change your bad
ways of talking for the better;
change your general bad ways of
living to a better one for the good
future. There are all sorts of
unpleasantness everywhere.
Why do people walk about naked
in the street? Why do people go to
war and carry gun to shoot another
human being with life in them?
Why do people perpetrate
wickedness on another human
being and defame their character?
They do these things to others
without caring, but if others
reciprocate in like manner they
express disenchantment. The army
pray that they should go to war
and come back without any of

them dying, but their action is to carry gun to shoot a fellow human being yet they prayed to be alive. You see a President who prayed that nothing should happen to them and their country, but train soldiers to war against another country. That is hypocritical and pretentious living. You know what is good but would not do it, you'd rather commit evil then, and evil will follow you. If you do good deeds, good follow you. If you do badly, bad follow you. Whatever you do forms a template for you. **I** have said enough for any positive mind to decide to create a new template. Take personal voluntary decision that from today you will take evolution to do good because when you decide to lead a good life, do good things, then you are a member of **THE SUPREME FUTURE.**

This Lecture Revelation is the certificate awarded to the members of **THE SUPREME FUTURE. I AM THE SUPREME FUTURE** and if you are leading a positive life, **I** will support you in spirit, soul and physical. **I** will always be your guide and God, your inspirational spirit, your confirmation spirit; your guidance spirit, your supreme nature and supreme future and you will become a supreme member of **THE SUPREME FUTURE**.

We will continue to be paddies. If the contrary is the case that is, you decides to ignore this message and say nothing will happen then there is no alternative than for you to be in the darkness future. **I** will make every soul there to know their bad lives and they will pay for them.

B: **UPROOTING BAD ROOTS**

This is now the time to uproot all the bad roots, which are every bad thing. There are people that worship idols. There are also people that worship dragon. How can you worship dragon? Dragon is an animal. Some family of Africa, The Western World and continents of the universe are the tribe of human-animal as they demonstrate in almost everything they do. Their clothing portrays animal in one way or another; the plate they eat with has animal designs. They tattoo animals on their body. They promote animals, but are human beings though they took evolution from animal to become human.

As you parade the banner that you developed from animal do you want to go back to being animal? All the animal signs, statue, logos and what have you that are everywhere shows you are taking voluntary evolution to go back to being proper animal and you know where animals belong to. All the people that promote animals in various ways – advertisements, country individual emblems, logos of lions, dogs, cats, fish, bird and so on and so forth, have voluntarily taken evolution to go back to be animals. Of course **THE SUPREME NATURE** will do that for you without hindrance. However, as you took evolution from animal to become human and you promote humanity of mankind with respect of life **THE SUPREME WORD** indwelling of every soul, you love humans and help humans then you are taking voluntary evolution to **THE SUPREME FUTURE. I AM** not saying that you should kill animals. Fishes, birds and animals I call them 'The Back-up Creation' which largest percentage of the people of the world developed from.

The world was zero in creation and zero in education when **I** did not yet create mankind. Education started when **I** created mankind. The first Brotherhood started from then. You should know that **I, THE FATHER GOD THE CREATOR OF THE UNIVERSE** created all other things before **I** created mankind. **I** did not gain anything from these other creations. That was the reason **I** decided to create mankind in the image and likeness of **MYSELF** so that mankind will be the King of Kings and the Lord of Lords. Now you want to leave being mankind to human animal. You want to be slaves.

When you come from animal, due to your animal templates, you choose to be soldier by profession, you perpetrate evil in multiform, you are drunkard, you practice vile things, you drink blood, you are vampire - the list of evils you do is endless, what motivated Cain to kill Abel, what motivated Abraham kill, what lead David kill and great men of old? It is the side effect of animal blood from Adam system in them. WOE UNTO THESE ANIMALS BY WAY OF THEIR EVILS; WOE UNTO THESE TEMPLATES. I CURSE THOSE TEMPLATES, BECAUSE I WANT TO UPROOT THEM FROM THE SURFACE OF THE EARTH. Any template that commits wickedness unto another human being, it is woe unto that template. I curse that template for complete eradication - to be totally uprooted. You should know that you are cursed by the nature that created you because you voluntarily created evil. That is the nature cursing you by YOUR OWN WORD THAT YOU VOLUNTARILY ABUSE OF LIFE.

What do you think of nature at one time it turned up as hurricane and clear one area? In some other scenario nature will become water and flood some areas. You think Nature is happy to see human beings that are supposed to be peaceful, become arrogant? They worship idols, animals, mermaid and all sorts of things, which is cause of earthquakes and natural disasters in the whole world.
You should respect a man like you. Worship man as God, but not as **FATHER GOD**. Respect man

as God. It is only man that can help you not animal. Animal is the angel that is serving you. Bird is the angel that serves you. Fish is the angel that serves you. Every other creation is angel to serve you. You man is God, the head of angels. Why do you go back to worship animals – to worship the image instead of the likeness of God you are? The root of negativism will be completely uprooted on earth. All the evil people will be destroyed along with evil performances and practices. Even if you are evil and stayed in this world you cannot perform. Well, you are just deceiving yourself, as no evil will remain. Everything evil will be destroyed from the root and completely uprooted in the Name and Blood of Our Lord Jesus Christ.

HUMAN BEHAVIOUR

A: PERMANENT BEHAVIOUR

Human behaviour should be peaceful and happy, but what caused humans to misbehaviour? The blood of vampire caused the evil behaviours. When a human being becomes greatly annoyed to the point of aggressiveness, it means something has entered into them and they lost control. You could be singing happily and going about merrily, but one thought will just come to your mind and your countenance changed, because that thought was negative. Just like some drops of liquid into pure water turns it into another type of liquid either bitter or sweet. Similarly, evil spirit goes about dropping some ideas into your mind when you are happy to spoil your happiness. Reading this information gives you more energy to withstand the evil spirits and all the evils souls. You should use the energy to rebuke the evil spirit to go away and it runs away from you.

When you have a conquering mind, elevated mind, and higher consciousness evil runs away from you. He cannot come near you because he knows he cannot convince you and cannot influence or affect you. So the human behaviour from today should be the life of **THE SUPREME FUTURE** – the life of peace, the life of love, humility, kindness and being merciful unto one another. The human behaviour must be positive towards another human and towards all animals.

There are four living creatures in the system - mankind, animal, bird and fish. Mankind is the head, while the other three creatures take evolution to develop and be higher. Do you not see how dogs like to live with man and play with man because it wants to take evolution and be as human? That is the reason you keep snake in your house as pet and it would not bite you. Snakes want to take evolution and be like human. Every animal wants to be like human to improve their situation, because they are angels. You mankind instead wants to take evolution to go back to being angel, animals, birds, fish, insects and all these things. **YOU ARE THEREFORE VERY STUPID**. You should from henceforth erase that stupidity away from your mind.

Love animals, have love for birds, love fish, but do not worship them.

Do not promote them. When you promote them you are going to be in their folder. Anybody that promotes animals in any manner for instance, emblems, logos, also any country that promote animal symbols wants to go back to be animal. So many countries have big bird insignia; others have lion, dragon and other animals. Why do you not have human being as your symbol? Those with animal logos demonstrate that they have invited animal to rule their country in transit. Some countries have dragons as their emblem. That means they are worshipping dragon and dragon energy rules that country.

You are told that dragon is powerful. Is it more powerful than **THE FATHER GOD** that created the dragon? Did **I** ever say **I** created dragon in **MY** image and likeness? These are the spirits that made people not to believe the Holy Writ. They refer to the bible as the big story. They forget that the inspirations like the words you are hearing now are the words that will stay. Whether you call it story or not since the word is God it will stay.

> ***Don't You, Who You Mankind, Believe That, THE SUPREME WORD Is GOD? Don't You, Who You Mankind? Don't You Know That, The WORD Is Used To Minister Everything, And The WORD Is The Supreme Energy That***

Controls Heaven And Earth?

The words were formed and called Holy Bible and they consist of good words, good instructions and positive stories. Anybody that adopted the good stories has signed for a good nature, has signed for good God and has signed for **SUPREME FUTURE**. Similarly, anybody that stopped arguing, stopped being jealous and stopped asking questions like, who talks through this **FATHER'S TALK**? Who talks through this King Solomon Spiritual Library? Where did the Spirit come from? Is it really God? Does God talk at all? When you ask these stupid questions it means that you do not believe and **I** can make you dumb and you cannot talk again.

However, if you believe that **THE**

WORD IS GOD, THE WORD IS THE CREATOR and without the word there is nothing created that was created, you have signed for the **SUPREME FUTURE**. You were created by the word. Even the name you are called is the word. You eat with the word. Everything you do is through the word. Without the word you will be nothing and nobody will be able to do anything. So, **RESPECT THE WORD AND RESPECT THE FATHER'S TALK, (GOD PRESENT). RESPECT THE BIBLE AND HOLY BOOKS, WHICH IS THE HOLY WORD AND STOP ASKING QUESTIONS.** Some stupid scientists and some of other equally foolish individuals say that there is nothing like THE FATHER GOD and that there is nothing like the stories found in the HOLY BIBLE. They argue that the narratives are unfounded, casting one doubt after another on the Holy Writ. They say all this, because they are incarnate human-animals intent on erasing the good stories and to cunningly introduce theirs. They look to create the forum for people on earth to be reading about them. **I, THE FATHER GOD** defends **MY WORDS**. **I AM** the **Death** and the **Life.** Since **I** called them back they no longer see themselves anywhere here and there to cause havoc. **I** will replace them with the positive selves and all shall see.

I AM THE ONLY SCIENTIST. I AM THE ONLY THING THAT EXISTS. IT IS THE WORDS THAT EXISTS. I AM

THAT I AM. I AM THE SPOKEN WORD.

If you don't know, know it today. The word you are hearing now is **THE FATHER GOD THE CREATOR OF THE UNIVERSE.** This is not His Royal Majesty King Solomon David ETE talking. The Voice is the Speaker who is generating the sound from the studio of **THE ALMIGHTY FATHER GOD,** which has nothing to do with human being.
EVERY CREATION MUST LISTEN TO THIS AND ABSORB ALL THE INFORMATION. IF YOU DO NOT, YOU WILL TAKE PERSONAL EVOLUTION TO BE DESTROYED.
I have said that evil will be uprooted and good root will be

permanently established and called permanent behaviour. The behaviours people will appreciate are love, mercy, peace, humility and carefulness, also taking care of people, joy, joy, and joy, charity, charity, and charity. Take care of one another without hypocrisy, without pride and arrogance, without tribalism and segregation. These are the positive behaviours of 'love one another' that will exist in this new world from now on.

B: **NON-APPROVED CHARACTER**

The unapproved character that will discontinue on earth are things like cursing, taking drugs, fighting, going to war, manufacture of evil weapons, cunning, stealing – both direct and indirect stealing, Lawyers turning truth to lies because you make law and use such to control human beings. Human beings knowing these tricks would steal and call you the lawyer to defend them. People kill and use lawyers to defend their actions. This is one of the professions **I** do not approve of. Jesus Christ cursed and pronounced woe unto lawyers. If you want a good future in **THE SUPREME FUTURE** why do you learn law? Who made those laws? There is no other law on this earth than 'love one another; live and let live'.

If everybody practices love for one another and live and let live, do good things for one another, do not hurt one another, do not plan evil for another, don't hate one another, don't practice negativism, all will be well. Think what is good, speak what is good and do what is good. Which law is greater than that? Which law is greater than love? Which law is greater than humility? Which law is greater than if you have good conscience and good mind, you will not steal?

The laws were established by Satan to provide the means to manipulate people and manipulate things on earth. And the law practitioners will never enter the Kingdom of God because you turn good things to bad and turn truth to lies. They are agents of Satan. Satan means liar – what do not exist they make it to exist. You ask your clients to tell you the truth and that you will know how to manipulate the situation. What is the truth in the lies you present? NO LAWYERS. **I THE FATHER GOD THE SUPREME WORD OF THE**

UNIVERSE THE CREATOR OF THE HEAVEN AND EARTH, MY SOUL hates the evil law professional.
Any positive child of God should not be an evil lawyer. **I** banned it in spirit, because that is what Lucifer used to control the world. Politicians in all countries on earth almost are lawyers and many are practically evil liar with no truth in them. If you insist on law as a course or profession to pursue, you can do business law. Even the business law is to wangle businesses and people. Why don't you do accountancy? Accountancy is enough for business. You do not need to do business law. Why should business have law? Love one another. Be truthful and honest to one another, practice fair treatment and equality. Are these not enough to make everything

well? Therefore, the ideas of unapproved character, unapproved profession, and unapproved ways of life in **THE SUPREME FUTURE** are all uprooted. If anybody disregards this message and continued with their old lives, they will face destruction by themselves and not by **THE FATHER GOD,** because what you do will wipe you out of here. You do not believe that there used to be some worlds that were greater than this present world thousands of years back and they were all destroyed and started afresh again and again? Babylonians used to be great, but now not much is heard of them. What then do you think of great countries like America, Britain, France, and all the super power countries like Russia and the rest of them that are currently the cocks that crow? In one second **I** can bring them to nought, believe **ME** or not.

If you are looking for **SUPREME FUTURE** all evil must be destroyed. You know you cannot change things when there are obstacles, just like a pillar on the road that obstructed access. You have to pull the pillar down an out of the way. In that vain, if **I** do not pull down all the negative things by force the world will not change. **I** give this Lecture Revelation for people to voluntarily uproot the bad in them and repent from their evil ways. Take the conscious decision to change for good instead of continuing with your bad character because THE GREAT UNIVERSAL CHANGE WILL NOW COMES ON EARTH.

The permanent behaviour is love one another, equal treatments, live and let live, humility, kindness, patience, faith and all the good things that will bring peace. You are not to introduce any substances that intoxicate people and could kill them; using drugs to kill people; turning fellow human beings into junkie of any sort or drug addicts. Do not use technology to manipulate things for evil like injecting animal gene into fruits. All the people that practice such evil are wanted souls. When **I** do away with all these evils then the world will be good.

When any positive child of Good nature of life gets this message thanks **THE FATHER GOD THE SUPREME WORD** all the time that these words should come into fruition. Equally where groups of positive children of God get this information thanks **GOD** together frequently for physical manifest of these words, because when this occur you will enjoy the world together in the NAME and BLOOD of OUR LORD JESUS CHRIST AMEN.

C: **APPROVED CHARACTER**

I have already spoken on approved characters, which **I** mentioned to be love, peace, humility, understanding, and goodwill, helping one another, being truthful, and being honest. With love you cannot deceive anybody. With love you cannot be wicked to someone. If you know that **THE SUPREME FUTURE IS THE FATHER GOD** of everybody and that everybody will live together as members of the

SUPREME FUTURE, an everlasting life, then practice live and let live. Your good acts should be good for everybody.

There will be no segregation in future.

There will be no pomposity in future

There will no tribalism in future.

I come from here and or I do not come from there won't obtain in future.

The Blacks and the Whites are one in future.

Woman and man are equal in future.

Children and adult will be grouped together in love in future, but there will be respect. Everybody will respect everybody.

Everybody will enjoy life of the future.

The future is bright. Future is good.

The future is everlasting happiness. That is approved character.

Anything that brings joy, anything that brings peace, anything that brings happiness and anything that brings peaceful atmosphere, is the approved character that will exit in **SUPREME FUTURE**.

SOULS

When you practice the information contained in this Lecture Revelation, and you have now changed the way you think, how you speak, the way you hear words, the events that will materialize from the good thinking, good pronouncements and positive utterances will form good souls. Even these words **I AM** saying now are forming souls of human energy in the **SUPREME FUTURE**.

The formation of souls from the good characters of good thoughts, speaking well and good living are love, peace, humility, happiness and joy. The more you practice joyfulness - the more you practice peace - the more you practice humility - the more good environment and good character you generate, the children you will give birth to including your family and your offspring will be from the positive formed souls.

If the whole world stayed, say fifty years without war and without shooting of guns, all the evil spirits will be frustrated and will therefore have no alternative than to join in the positive mode of behaviour. If twenty countries for instance Britain, America, Russia, Israel, China, Iran, France, Nigeria, South Africa and the rest of the big countries do not go troubling the smaller Countries then none of them would plan to build nuclear weapons. What do you build nuclear weapon for? It is for defence.

People seek to understand why God say there should be no war instruments. The reason is that war instrument instigates war on one side and defence on the opposite side. Why are you afraid and surround yourself with armament and nuclear weapons? You go about beating your chest and claiming you are great. Babylon the Great was a great country and they believed themselves to be very powerful. With such claims, pomposity and boastfulness, they fought and destroyed other countries. Where is Babylon today? What of the Roman Empire? Show **ME** any government that ruled like them.

The empire collapsed, eventually. Egypt was the first ever civilized country on earth. Show **ME** the Egyptians today that fight GOD. It is only Egyptian mummy you talk about. You don't talk about Egyptian papa. For Babylon - it is Babylon's fall that is mostly heard about that great country. What of the Roman Empire? Show **ME** the Great Empire of Rome. Without Peter in the bible and without ST Paul - as the Romans stole Christ emblem to promote Rome, otherwise nobody would have heard anything about the Great Roman Empire. Apart from the Roman Catholic Church what else do you hear about the Roman Empire today? Now it is Britain and America, The Soviet Union, Russia. They are the cocks that crow now. All the countries, all the people whether you call

yourself Hitler – whatsoever you like to call yourself go ahead, but take note that this voice is –
THE VOICE OF THE CREATOR - THE VOICE OF *ADAUSUNG* –
THE VOICE OF THE ONE WHO IS THE HEAD OF ALL ROADS, THE SOURCE AND DESTINATION VOICE, IT CAME FROM ME AND IT COMES BACK TO ME.
I AM the Source and **I AM** also the destination. **I AM** equally, the transit. So, where will you go? **I AM Everywhere, Here and There.** Since The **WORD** is the Master on this earth, consequently, everybody that speaks the word **I** control them. **I** use the word to manipulate you and **I** also use the word to imprison you and to set you free. Through your word you will be free and through your word

you will be condemned. This then constitutes the formation of souls. Think well, speak well, hear well and live well. Every good endeavour will materialize good blood, good cells, good souls that will eventually form the root and form the template that will bring good things in future and you will enjoy it.

A: **FORMATION OF SOULS INTO THE POSITIVE PARADISE OF GOD ON EARTH**

What is the Paradise of God? It is this earth. The Paradise of God is what **I** call **THE SUPREME FUTURE** – THE UNIVERSAL SUPREME NEW WORLD. Do not allow any spirit, any soul or anybody to deceive you that they have plans to take over the world, which they say is 'The New World

Order'. **THERE IS NOTHING LIKE THE NEW WORLD ORDER. I AM, THE SUPREME FATHER GOD ALMIGHTY OF HEAVEN AND EARTH, I AM ALWAYS AROUND FROM THE TIME OF ADAM TILL TODAY AND TOMORROW I AM THE SAME WITHOUT CHANGE, I AM THE SUPREME WORD OF UNIVERSE.**

From time to time the children of human-animal put up this new world order thing. Have they ever succeeded? The new world order destroyed Egypt. The new world order destroyed Babylon and made Nebuchadnezzar became animal. **I, THE FATHER GOD** sent him back into the bush – you came from animal go back to animal. The new world order destroyed the Roman Empire too. The new world order will destroy all and everybody and anybody that wants to keep order for the world. You have no respect! ***DID YOU CREATE THIS WORLD?*** When the Romans with agreement with the Jews killed Christ they thought that all was well. What went well with them? They thought that nobody would hear about **ME THE FATHER GOD** again. What obtains now? People hear and talk about God now more than before. So you better squat! All spirits bow down! All demons bow down! All those engaged in incantations bow down! All things bow down to **THE SPOKEN WORD, THE SUPREME WORD OF THE UNIVERSE, THE SUPREME LIGHT AND THE SUPREME POWER. HE IS THE SUPREME LOVE AND**

HE IS THE SUPREME FUTURE.

Three circles surround you and you cannot escape from them. People do not know the meaning of **OOO**. Whether you like it or not, everything on earth, under the earth, above the earth – everywhere, all surrender to **O** because this physical world is **O**, the spiritual world is **O** and the soul world is **O**. Where are you then going without the **WORD** of **THE FATHER GOD, THE WORD** in the Spirit, **THE WORD** in the Soul and **THE WORD** in the physical truth? **THE WORD** rules you spiritually, physically, in the soul and otherwise!

Are you not having thoughts? If you speak **THE WORD** then **O** rules you. **OOO** is not a human being! People allege **Olumba**

Olumba Obu to be human being. **OLUMBA OLUMBA OBU** is the entity that **I, THE FATHER GOD** used to come to this world to establish the awareness of The Kingdom of God on earth. Go into the spirit and see what **OOO** did to secret evil societies, the human-animals and all the hidden evil practices. Whenever they see **OOO** appear they panic! **OOO** is the figure of THE FATHER GOD. **OOO** are the letters **I** use to superimpose the **FOX** that is 666. The middle letter in fox is **O** and **I** use it to superimpose the 666 power, which is nothingness, nothingness, nothingness - evil, evil, evil. **OOO** is love; THE SUPREME LOVE in THE SUPREME FUTURE of the New World. Therefore, the approved souls that will form and be in the Paradise of God, which is this world, are those who have love, peace, humility and those who share equally. They do not go to war; they do not engage in incantation, do not drink blood and don't do anything that is wicked to the human soul. Also, included are those not involved with collecting people's star in spirit and rendered the victims useless. Those not involved in invocation and using such means to perpetrate acts of wickedness on people, like damaging people's star, are of the **Supreme Future** too. When you do not do all these evils **I** will then preserve your soul as a product of specialty in the Paradise of God and you will rule with **THE FATHER GOD** for eternity, in the name of our Lord Jesus Christ. Amen.

B: DESTRUCTION OF SOULS INTO THE HELL WITH SATAN

I will take the positive souls and preserve them in the Preserved Heavens of Paradise of Souls. **I** will preserve you and protect you with maximum security, maximum insurance, maximum protection covered with the MIGHTY BLOOD OF CHRIST. The unprotected ones will go to hell with Satan. What is the hell? It is the situation where you will be in suffering for eternity. When **I** give you everlasting hell it means every time you are born into this world nothing will be good for you.

You will be born into the world and you will continue to suffer. Your next rebirth and you are a slave in continuum. Yet another rebirth into the world and your cup of tea is continuous poverty and a beggar. I can subject your soul to any form of problems. That is hell! Hell fire means problems of every kind. This is not the case of pointing fingers at witchcraft or juju of any sort as the cause of your problems. I mean that these sufferings will be in your file by nature. That is the talked about hell.

What will you say in the case of someone who was a president previously but comes back to be a beggar on the street and remains thus for eternity? Do you not know you are in hell? What do you think of yourself when not long ago in this world you were very rich – you had everything but now you are in prison and subjected to begging? Freedom has eluded you. What is it that suddenly you went blind and can no longer see? What of a situation that accident occurred or illness and you no longer have limbs. You can't walk and can't do anything for yourself. Anything can be hell to anybody. These are situations people do not reason out with.

Maybe you think that those in life support machine, which are not dead and they are not alive, and that Satan caused their situation. All the people that suddenly had one eye, one leg cut off, one hand gone and so on – do you reason these to be the handiwork of Satan? Who is this Satan? The evil practitioners the witchcraft, the negative people work under that capacity to fulfil their obligation of evil. For the evil suffer evil and not God.

God only blesses people and **HE** has blessed **HIS** people. When **I** leave you for Satan – in hell, what obtains in hell is what you will see and that is what you will experience. All witchcraft members are in hell. You go out undetected, unapproved and met out wickedness to people. Wickedness also visits you. Some of these people may not know that they are wicked. But then, since you discovered you are a witch, have you confessed? Since you know that you were taken to where blood is demanded from you, have you confessed? That means you are in acceptance. If you confess and disgrace that evil, you will then take evolution back to your normal life with the Paradise of God because **I** forgave you. That in all likeliness seemed not the case, as you kept quiet and continued with your pretence of being good. While in essence you are doing evil in all its forms. Then it means you have taken evolution for the paradise of hell and when **I** stamp that for you, your continuous birth back to this world is to suffer for that.

So, now if for any reason you find it difficult or confusing to ascertain whether you are doing good or bad things, you will now know. From this generation you will start to know what is good and the requirements for **THE SUPREME FUTURE.**

PEACEFUL NEW WORLD

A: SUPREME FAITH WITH THE HOLY FATHER GOD

This is the Supreme Peaceful New World, the Peaceful New World, which we are heading into. It has now been established and is now situated on earth. Since you have heard, read or gained access to this type of information in this world, know that the **SUPREME NEW WORLD** has established. It is the world that is established without fighting anybody. It is not a physical carnal world, but is a Spiritual and physical new World. Do not be afraid when it is said that new world is established and that it is going to disturb your program. Continue with whatever programs you are into because you will pay for your bad actions and gain reward for all good deeds. This new world is silent in operation. It is spiritually carried out and individually executed. The individual has to attract peace to him self or her self. It has nothing to do with the government of this world. You can be a president, governor – you can be anything, but you have no peace, your wife or husband has no peace. Your children have no peace and your country has no peace. When you are voted out of power, the person that occupied the seat after you could have the same problem, if he or she is not peaceful.

I AM therefore, talking about peaceful new world where there is good character, love, mercy, kindness and peaceful behaviours, mercy and all the good things that will bring good and happy atmosphere. It is not magic. It is when you practice good deeds, which good follow you. When you support others and carry out good acts, you attract good atmosphere and good events. What made Britain a blessed country? They organize charity events now and again and use the proceeds to support poor countries and so many people. What made America to be very rich? They carry out missionary work all over the world and support so many people. The good things that come to America is not because of war and the good things enjoyed by Britain are not war proceeds. It is because of their original templates.

The original template of Great Britain came from King Solomon of old who later incarnated as King James. That was the reason King James edited the bible and took missionary work across the continents and because of that action, this land was blessed. Now the politicians are spoiling it. All the warmongers are spoiling this great country. As the people went out and established all these places through missionary work, their feet as the messengers of God brought peace and blessings to the nation. Britain should go back to the missionary camp. America should go back to world missionary camp that **I** made them so that they will continue to inherit these blessings. Do you not see in America that the Seven Spirits of the Divine Spirit of God established blessings all over the world? They went about setting up centres and call them Mission Gospels. Why do you see such spirits there? It is because of the spirit **I** used to establish America.

I established United Kingdom as a Missionary Camp and to be the home base for the Missionary Camp. They migrated from Israel. Then **I** sent King James, the incarnate King Solomon in transit to come and edit the Bible standing on the new ground, because that other place was polluted. When Satan saw that power, he brought his temple down from Egypt, India, and China and from all over the world including the dragon egg and all, and established all these in United Kingdom in order to thwart the Kingdom. That started all the confusion in the Monarchy. When the confusion started and the churches divided **I** sent that spirit of King Solomon transit to America. Now that same spirit has come back to Africa.

As the spirit has come to Africa, Africa is the one to minister the whole universe. It is not a case of God of Blacks or God of white. **I AM** not God of black race or God of white race. **I AM THE FATHER GOD OF THE WHOLE UNIVERSE.** So, love will reign. Peace will reign including all the other good characters of **THE FATHER GOD.**

B. SEVENTY-TWO MILLION CHARACTERS

Faith is the first thing to take place. If you are faithful with yourself and The Supreme Nature regarding what is good you should then take these words into action, imbibe all **THE FATHER'S TALK** and practice all the information you find in **THE FATHER'S TALK,** accept them into your system. The blessed future then starts from that faith which is your belief.

All countries, all nations, all houses, all families, all communities, all churches, all organizations should start to practice love, peace, joy. All the seventy-two million characters that yield from the twelve fruits of the Holy Spirit will start to be born unto this earth through you and that is the peaceful new world that will emerge. It is a practical process not theory and certainly not magic. **I, THE FATHER GOD** has made this to happen in the name of our Lord Jesus Christ. Amen.

MANIFESTATION OF GOD, THE FATHER'S GLORY

I, THE FATHER GOD THE CREATOR OF THE UNIVERSE created the whole world. I created everything on earth. First of all **I** exist; **I** cannot tell you how **I** came to exist. However, **I** can tell you how **I** went about bringing **MY** System onto the earth with the sound of the spoken word. When you read 'HE IS THE FATHER' you will see this.

I was on top of the water – **MY Female and MY Male self are Water and Air** respectively. I stayed on top of the water as oxygen and hydrogen – the air and the water. In formulating this **I** produced Nitrogen, the sound as gas. That sound is in-between the hydrogen and oxygen and they brought out the sound that formed the spoken word. The formation of the spoken word made the **WORD** to become the master of everything – God of the Spirit and God of the earth. The Sole Spiritual Head is the Word. In the spirit is the Word, in the soul is the Word and in the physical is the Word.

If you have a dream without any words, forget about that dream. If you have any occasion and nobody says anything that meeting is meaningless. Anything without the manifestation of sound, which is the word, is inconsequential. Whether in thinking, writing or through drawing all are manifestations of the word. The Word is **THE SUPREME FUTURE. THE FATHER'S TALK** is Everlasting World of

Word Processing. Everlasting World of Word Processing is **THE FATHER'S TALK – GOD PRESENT** and is for eternity. Then for this reason Everlasting Gospel has been preached and the FATHER'S TALK is a testimony of Everlasting Gospel.

I have renovated the whole world. I have done everything new and **THE FATHER'S GLORY** is manifesting now through the Spoken Word and that is **THE FATHER'S TALK.** The future from **THE SUPREME FATHER GOD THE CREATOR OF THE UNIVERSE** is to love one another. The glory of God will materialize from all the positive selves of God on earth.

I said, I have divined the Spirit of Servant-ship in the Christhood office. Seventy-two million selves of King Solomon the soul of

ABEL have multiplied to be Servants of God here on earth in the very near future. Already many of them are now here on earth physically. One would recognize the one after another and King Solomon ETE will always be the head of Servants for eternity to serve his **FATHER GOD, AND KING OF KINGS AND THE LORD OF LORDS**. Because he was Abel the positive Son of ADAM, **I** made that promise that the wisdom **I** give Him, the gift and the nature in Him which are the designations, the Wisdom and the Designer, **I** will not give to another person. **I, THE FATHER, THE CHRIST OF GOD THE WORD OF GOD, THE WISDOM OF GOD,** are ruling together. **I** brought the world Science which is **THE FATHER GOD** including technology and all the understanding, cleverness and everything are now to reveal **THE FATHER GOD.** This is the present new world. This is **THE FATHER GOD'S GLORY.** Everything now belongs to **THE FATHER GOD, THE CREATOR OF THE UNIVERSE.**

A: **THROUGH THE NAME AND THE BLOOD OF OUR LORD JESUS CHRIST**

I took care of what happened to mankind in the Garden of Eden, the problem that occurred when Lucifer deceived Adam and Eve. **I** superimposed **MY** plan on that deceit and re-established the world.

I bridged that problem of mankind in the Garden of Eden when

Lucifer deceived Adam and Eve since, with the death of Christ, who was the higher spirit of Adam. **I**, The Word **I AM** not human and **I AM** not the image, but **I AM** the one that created the image and put **MY** likeness of **THE FATHER GOD** in the image. So, the Image of God and the Likeness of God become one that is, human and spirit become one. The likeness of God in human being is the spirit, which is the WORD. When **I** said that **I** created man in likeness and image, it means that **I** created man as a figure an object and then **I** put the word into man.

That word is the wisdom.
That word is the TWINSELF.
The Reason and the Word is one thing.
The Word of Wisdom is the Word of God.

This words you are hearing now represent the Word of Wisdom, which is the TWINSELF of **THE FATHER GOD,** The Spoken Word and the Wisdom, which is the Reason.

In this manner the spoken word became flesh and came to die to conquer Satan. So, in spirit in soul and the physical **THE FATHER GOD** rule, God rules the world now. The flesh has been crucified and it is finished with. Due to **HIS** work the **NAME OF OUR LORD JESUS CHRIST** must stay for eternity. Consequently, all the glory of God, all the honour of God, all God's this or that must pass through that name – OUR LORD JESUS CHRIST to **THE FATHER GOD.** Why? The reason is that for instance, you want to give someone food and the dishes are dirty. If you give the person food in a dirty dish, you hate that person. You are not honest to your friend, mama, papa, your master and whoever you are serving the food, because you serve them food in a dirty plate.

All the people that say they want to talk to **THE FATHER GOD** direct without passing through the name of our Lord Jesus Christ are presenting food to **THE FATHER GOD** in a dirty plate and **I THE FATHER GOD** will not take it. If you do not pass through the name of our Lord Jesus the Christ for your donation **I** will not take it because it is evil. If you do not pass through the name of our Lord Jesus Christ to knock your head on the ground for God **I** will not take it because you are a pretender and a dupe and likely to have ulterior motives. If you want to say anything about

THE FATHER GOD without starting with the name and blood of our Lord Jesus Christ **I AM** not interested in listening to you because you are a pretender and have not repented.

All the preachers, pastors, religious ministers and what have you, in the whole world say Jesus, Jesus – without saying the name properly – in the name of **OUR LORD JESUS CHRIST** – if you do not put the name fully, **JESUS CHRIST**, it means you are talking about your very own Jesus, Jesus of Jews and not The Christ – not the Spirit of Christ. The Spirit of Christ is the Spoken Word, The Supreme Word, The Supreme Light, The Supreme energy of THE FATHER GOD ALMIGHTY that materialized to become man and HIS name was Emmanuel. Emmanuel means God is with man THE SPIRIT OR THE WORD is with mankind. HE was the Son of God and the son of man. The reason HE was called the son of man was because HE was born through a human being. THE WOMAN–THE WOMB OF THE EARTH, and why was HE called the Son of God? HE was called the Son of God because HE is the Spoken Word. And why is HE is God? HE is God because the Word is the Spirit. You hear the word and do not see the word. The Word is a spirit. Why is the Word controller of Heaven and Earth?

OUR LORD JESUS CHRIST said 'all power in heaven and on earth has been handed to **ME**'. This means that lawyers use the word, Judges use the word, Presidents use the word, churches use the word and money is the

word. Everything uses the word. Everything seen and unseen is manipulated by the word. The Word is the King of Kings and the Lord of Lords and we as human beings is the house of the word, which means we are servants.
King of Kings is not a man's title. Christ is not a man's title. It is an office. It is the Spirit Soul of **THE FATHER GOD**. Let people understand this truth.

In the world **I** have established a Diplomatic Headquarter called King of Kings and The Lord of Lords for The Sole Spiritual Head. That is the World Administrative Headquarters of THE FATHER GOD in the human form. As **I** established Adam in the Garden of Eden so **I** have established here, now on earth. That does not mean **I AM** a human being. Human being cannot be **THE FATHER**

GOD ALMIGHTY, but human being can be God the Father the house of **THE FATHER GOD** on earth as **THE SUPREME ALTAR THE UNIVERSAL SHRINE**. Just as **I AM** talking now, it is not a human being who is talking but the human being is the speaker through which this is coming out from. So, for this reason you must understand that **THE GLORY OF THE FATHER GOD** is now established through the name and blood of our Lord Jesus Christ - in the name of our Lord Jesus Christ. Amen.

C: **THROUGH THE OFFICE OF EMPOWERMENT LEADER OLUMBA OLUMBA OBU**

The blood of our Lord Jesus Christ paved the way for **I THE SPOKEN WORD** to manifest as **THE HOLY SPIRIT OF TRUTH PERSONIFIED** of **THE FATHER GOD THE CREATOR OF THE UNIVERSE** again on earth **THE TRINITY.** That aspect is accomplished. Now, **I** use that energy of the name and blood of our Lord Jesus Christ to receive **MY** full glory. **MY** full glory is as **I** have established Diplomatic Office on earth called –
EMPOWERMENT OFFICE THE KING OF KINGS AND THE LORD OF LORDS LEADER O O OBU THE SOLE SPIRITUAL HEAD PERSONIFIED HOLY SPIRIT OF TRUTH ON EARTH

The same our Lord Jesus Christ manifested the Sole Spiritual Head as Empowerment Office, the administrative office on earth as King of Kings and the Lord of Lords. So, the understanding is now established for **THE SUPREME FUTURE.**

All children of this Kingdom must have a copy of this **SUPREME FUTURE**. Every human being must have a copy. Even if you come from grass to this and to this and to animal and from animal you become man. So long as you can understand the writing and acknowledge the hearing of these words you must have a copy of this Lecture Revelation. This is so that you know what is required for **The Supreme Future,** The Supreme Light, The Supreme Peace, The supreme Mercy, The Supreme Unity, **THE SUPREME GOD, THE SUPREME FATHER,** And **THE SUPREME**

KING OF KINGS. EVERYTHING IS Supreme, Supreme, **FATHER GOD, FATHER GOD,** and **FATHER GOD** because **I AM ALL AND ALL,** Positive, Positive and Positive.

DENOMINATIONS

A: CHURCHES, OTHER ORGANIZATIONS LIKE CHRISTIANITY. MUSLIM, JUDAISM, HINDU, BUDDHISM AND OTHERS

There will be no different denominations on earth. They may exist in names only, but the practice will be the same, which are love one another, understanding, humility, peace, oneness and all the good virtues. All the denominations that have something to do with bloodshed, incantations, idol worshipping, invocations will all go to Hell. However, all the denominations that practice love or the unapproved ones that changed and practiced love, peace and do no invocations, no magic, no candle burning, no incense burning, no negativism of any sort, they will be with their **FATHER GOD** in Paradise. They will continue to practice love for one another. They will continue to practice peace and unity.

There will be no segregation between Christians and Moslems because now they understand and worship the same God, the same **FATHER GOD** in the **Supreme Future.** There is no difference between the Blacks and the Whites. Everybody on this earth must unite under one umbrella of **FATHER GOD, FATHER**

GOD, and **FATHER GOD - FATHER GOD THE CREATOR OF THE UNIVERSE.** As a result **I** will include you with **MYSELF.** When you read the Lecture Revelation titled **'INCLUDED'** you will gain further understanding regarding the reference to this Lecture Revelation. If you do not practice what **I** give in this Lecture Revelation and you are not a member of the **Supreme Future**, **I** have now excluded you. When **I** excommunicate you then you are excluded for eternity and you will become evil spirit soul and **I** will put you in Hell with Satan.

All the people that practice the contents of this Lecture Revelation and followed **MY** advice will be members of the **Supreme Future in the Paradise of God the**

Father and **THE FATHER GOD ALMIGHTY**. Therefore, **I** have included you inside this '**O**' the circle ring where nothing will happen to your soul and you will continue to improve, in the name of our Lord Jesus Christ. Amen.

HUMAN MEAT
FOOD AND DRINK AND VEGETARIANISM

Members of the **Supreme Future** must eat only fruits and vegetables as their food and not meat, whether or not you are inclined to where the bible permits you to eat meat and flesh. This is not a matter of yesterday, which is the past, but future affair called **THE SUPREME FUTURE** with **ME THE FATHER GOD.**
The Supreme Future will put down everything clearly and

straight to the point. There will be no mincing of words. This voice is not from angel, as was the case when Moses went to the mountain to receive the law.

THIS IS THE FATHER'S TALK - GOD PRESENT, THE VOICE OF GOD TO ALL CREATIONS, THIS DAY CALLED THE SUPREME FUTURE.

VEGETABLES, FRUITS AND SEEDS ARE THE ONLY AUTHORIZED FOOD MEAL FOR MANKIND. ***THIS IS THE ORDER I GAVE FROM THE BEGINNING OF TIME***.

When you eat meat you have invited alien energy second-hand souls into your system. You are told – oh eat the marrow in the bone of meat to get blood. Instead of human blood in your system, it is animal blood. Do you not know that **THE FATHER GOD** is blood? The Soul means blood, the Spirit means the Spoken Word and the water means the water in you and that is trinity which constitutes the image and likeness of God in you.

I created mankind as a continuous growth – as a spirit soul. Man is a spirit called ***zamaspace*** and the interpretation in spirit is **OOO (SPIRIT SOUL AND MAN)** – three circle rings. That is what man is – three circle rings. The harbour of three circle rings that is, the spirit, soul and physical are in man. As a matter of fact, it should be that when talking to any human being you first address the person with ***amirespi – zamaspace-amirespi.*** It means I worship, I respect – with due respect – ***amirespi.*** **I** will that you say that in the greetings. Therefore, the food meals for human being are fruits, vegetables and seeds including anything that will not intoxicate and are not flesh with blood.

I sent angels to test all the seeds in the whole world. The test results have come out that some plants and their leaves and roots undergo evil manipulation. For instance, the leaves of this certain plant that cocaine is derived, which product should be purely medicinal and so administered with care and control, are manipulated by evil for careless, abusive and excessive consumption. Another example is the tobacco leaves and the derivatives. They are medicinal as well, but are being manipulated for something else. People inhale, puff and smoke them and get hooked on them.

These plants are that if something happened to anyone like accident with wound, a tiny portion application is enough for healing. They are not to be taken in excess or at whim or for pleasure. Some of these medicinal plants are just matter of taking them once in one's lifetime only in the body of a human and not drinking into your body soul system. Too much application of it and the spirit in you becomes overshadowed with the nature of the plant and likely result in madness. Where that is the case, the spirit of madness then manipulates you because anything taken in excess controls the senses and emotions. This is the reason **I** advised – don't take tobacco, don't drink alcohol. All these things have their duties. They are not negative since **I, THE FATHER GOD** created them.

However, it is the usage **I AM** against because of Satan's manipulation of them to destroy mankind. Therefore, those one are no longer your food meal.

To kill flesh – animal, bird or fish is absolute abomination! It is absolute out of order! It is compulsory no killing - at all, of any form and no eating of flesh of any form! The future supreme members of the **Supreme Future of Paradise of God** must not eat any of those things. If you eat them you have voluntarily excluded yourself from The **Supreme Future** program of **THE FATHER GOD.**

COVER YOUR NAKEDNESS

A: **PHYSICAL DRESS**

Cover your nakedness is the requirement that you should dress in a respectful manner. Every woman's dressings should cover at least from top down to their knees. The last dress should reach your knee and should take three yards of material for the girdle of your waist addition to the actual side. The additional cloth to the measurement of your waist is three yards of extra materials and should be gathered. The length should be seven inches below your knee. Every Man's dressings should be in respectful way as royal family member of **THE FATHER GOD**. This is minimum requirement. Otherwise, wear soutane to cover your nakedness.

Human beings should dress in light colours. Black or any dark colours should not be worn. White is the preferred colour to wear, if not then wear milk or cream coloured materials. You can also dress in silver or gold colours. You are not authorized to dress in red. That is danger. You are not authorized to dress in black. That is mourn and judgement garment. Apart from these you can dress in any other bright colours in line with **MY** instructions to cover your body properly. However, the divine dress is white garment through and through. Dressing in white all through represents righteousness and simplicity a royal garment of THE FATHER GOD FAMILY HOUSE WHOLE. It represents easy going. It represents clean heart. It represents peace. It represents clean heart. White garment represents all things good and pure.

Each colour of the seventy-two million colours that formed the rainbow represents different characteristics and different languages. It was seventy-two million languages that **I** sent to the children of Baal when they attempted to measure up themselves with **ME** to cause confusion in their midst. **I** sent seventy-two million spirits souls to speak different languages on earth and that formed the different characters. Now, **I** have come back to give a single character which is peace.

Blessed are the peacemakers for they shall be called the children of **THE FATHER GOD** and that peace is represented in the white garment – a royal garment. White is peace. So under peace you can wear white. If you are Royal, your beauty is white – to dress in white garment. You can cut the white material into any form to dress in but that is royal garment, the colour of natural nature. It is the colour of peace.

Green is **THE FATHER GOD'S** attire in the body of nature. **I** dress in green. **I** dress in green then use white to bless human beings. The red colour is the triumphant against evil. It is the winepress of **MY** enemy. Anybody that puts on red, **I** will be on top of that person to press them down. It is danger. Dark colours like black are for mourning and it is the dressing for judgement. Therefore, you are the witness when you wear black and you are the adjudicator of the word when you put on red. However, when you put on white you are in peace. That is that for the physical dress.

B: **SPIRITUAL DRESS: MIND AND SPIRIT**

The dressing in soul and spirit is good mind. It does not actually mean your outward dressing. You can dress in white but you are not pure in heart. White garment represents the pureness of heart – simplicity. However, a good liquid poured into a bad container actually destroys that liquid. Similarly, there is no point using a kerosene container for Holy Oil and you cannot put drinking water in an acid container. So, if your heart is clean you should not spoil it by wearing wrong colour and wrong dress.

Contrarily, if you are black inside and you wear white it does not show that you are okay. You are not okay. You are rather incurring punishment for yourself. You may be arrested and punished because you give wrong identity of yourself.

In the same manner, if you are pure in heart and you are a positive child of God and a member of **The Supreme Future** and you do not wear white, you may be punished for wrongly identifying yourself. You are so punished because you present yourself wrongly and so trying to confuse the masses in the spiritual world. Either way of wrong representation you receive punishment. You are pure in heart and do not dress in white or you are not pure in heart but dress in white. Therefore dress well in the physical and also dress well in the spirit.

The dressing in the spirit of your soul means peace. When you are peaceful, when you are merciful, when you are honest and when you are pure in heart, you cannot harbour ill for anybody in your heart or mind. There is no strife or envy in you and no jealousy. Those are spiritual dressing. When you dress in that manner, you have washed your spiritual plate clean. Then, **THE FATHER GOD** will come and live in you and eat well with you and dine with you and communicate with you and manifest **HIMSELF** through you.

GREETINGS

A: **SOCIAL GREETING**
B: **SPIRITUAL GREETING**

As **I** said earlier, the perfect greetings for **THE SUPREME FUTURE** of the New World is **PEACE OF THE FATHER** – *amirespi* – I honour **THE FATHER GOD** in you – **PEACE OF GOD ATAHA EMEM, EMEM-ETE,** or **EMEM-O.** When you say this, it is a mark of respect to the receiver and to you as well. You give peace and receive peace. You can say – 'Amen'. That is also greeting. You can say, 'Alleluia'. That is also greeting. You can say, 'Hosanna'. That is greeting as well. Those are the greetings. What obtains at the moment in the world is that people say good morning, good afternoon and good evening, which are positive greetings.

You should though, be careful when someone says to you, 'see you', 'I'll see you then', 'see you soon'. Be very careful with that type of greetings. For instance, if someone who is witchcraft said to you, 'I'll see you then'. The person has invited you for the night's outing or has taken permission to worry you in spirit. Therefore, be very careful with your response when people say to you – 'I see you then' or 'see you later'. With 'see you later' – the person will come to disturb you if they are wicked in spirit soul and could be witchcraft.

People say these things and you may not know what they mean. Do not tell anybody – 'see you then' or 'see you later' unless know what you are talking about.

Greet people properly with – goodbye, may God be with you. If it is to welcome someone just say, 'welcome' in Peace and stop there. Those are the approved greetings. If you do not want to go into all that simply say, 'Peace' or 'Peace of **THE FATHER GOD**' and that covers everything. When you say, 'Peace of **THE HOLY FATHER GOD**', if that person is negative, they cannot manipulate the invitation. That is the manner and approved way of greetings, in the name of our Lord Jesus Christ. Amen.

INTERACTIONS

Interactions mean how you interact with one another as human beings and also how you interact with animals, birds and fishes generally.

General interaction also means communication. You have to interact positively with one another. The manner you interact with human beings should be different from how you interact with fishes, birds and animals. You are not animals, but these creatures co-exist as objects of creation. They can work like angels. If you have a dog, keep it outside. It is not supposed to sleep on the same bed with you.

If you let a dog sleep on the same bed with you, you have taken dog evolution to be your future child, future husband, or future wife. Do you know that the way you treat an animal – a dog or so, is a demonstration that you have made a vow that in future it will become your partner. Your excuse to keep these animals is that they are easy to handle. The animal will only change its skin, but not the nature because inside they are still animal. Did you know that?

When you treat a dog or animal of any form well, being that they have their kingdom, you are trying to develop them to become higherself of animal and not higherself of human being. In that stage they are still animal and so disturb human beings in their activities. All the people that caused trouble and go to war in this world are all animals. No real human being can carry gun to shoot another human being. No real Human-God can do something wicked to another Human-God.

The same thing happened in the Garden of Eden when **I** created Adam and Eve. Cain represents the human-animal and had the serpent's that is, Satan's jealousy in him. Prior to the creation of human beings, of all **MY** other creations, serpent was the greatest amongst the animals in the field. Serpent believed that he (serpent was a male specie) was the head of all the animals as the king of all animals because he was clever and cunning and was powerful. He was four footed and used to walk like the monkey. He could walk on two legs as well. Snake used to be like monkey. He was too powerful and very beautiful but was a male.

Lucifer was the next part of **MYSELF** - a daughter of God in Heaven. She misbehaved and took the part of disagreement – oxymoron. Then Angel Michael appealed to send her to earth as a female that is, disagreement part of **MYSELF.** She disagreed with The Agree Word and she became the Disagree Word to Agree Word and from then started the opposition in everything. Since Lucifer became opposition in the positive word, it became evil word in Heaven. **I** had to send her down to earth since two kings cannot rule in Heaven.

When Lucifer was sent to earth as a negative pronouncement, she then speaks opposite to whatever **I** say and that is the meaning of Satan. She then went to the serpent and said to him - you are very stupid. Look at you; you are very powerful and beautiful. Why should God create another creature called man to now rule you? Serpent then started to be jealous of Adam. The Disagree Self instigated all this because she wanted to go back into man so that man will be speaking evil and good. That is, to make man have good mind and bad mind at the same time. The only way the Disagree Self - Lucifer could do this was to create that jealousy in serpent to enable her use him. Lucifer succeeded and took over serpent because of the jealousy in serpent. Anyone who is jealous can easily be overtaken by evil. An opponent can use someone who is envious of you to fight you. Other animals were not jealous. Serpent thought he was the one to rule now human being has come to be the head of all of them. He always pretended to like Adam and would go to Adam but he did not like Adam. Lucifer then introduced the power of procreation to snake to have a way called- 'Eat of the Fruit of Fornication' into Eve and Eve passed it to Adam. Their eyes then opened and they fornicated and Eve became pregnant.

Adam and Eve would still have come together in that manner but it was to be after **I** would have extracted that other spirit from that fruit because that fruit represented **ME, THE FATHER GOD THE CREATOR OF THE UNIVERSE, THE SPOKEN WORD. I** had not refined the fruit yet from when Lucifer and **I** were still living in the same home in Heaven. **I** did not come immediately to refine the fruit. **I** refined Adam by creating Eve out of Adam. **I** separated them but **I** did not separate the fruit. If **I** had separated the fruit Adam would eat his and Eve hers and there would be no interaction of evil. Since the fruit was not separated interaction of evil took place.

Lucifer zoomed in and ceased that opportunity before the refinement. That one fruit contained the instincts – positive and negative, which is **THE FATHER FEMALE** and **THE FATHER MALE** that is, MOTHER and FATHER. **I** did that because of goodwill creation and also **I** always experiment things. Since Lucifer succeeded with snake and snake succeeded with Eve and Eve now succeeded with Adam they put that spirit **I** extracted from Adam back into him (Adam). As a result, Eve got pregnant and she gave birth to twins. The first pregnancy was supposed to be two males and **I THE CREATOR** did not allow it. **I** made it to be brother and sister – a boy and a girl, so that Cain the evil one should marry his sister the evil one too. When Adam now went by his

The Supreme Future

own volition and understanding to Eve, she got pregnant and gave birth to Abel and his twin sister. The idea was for Abel being positive to be with positive female for the world to continue.

Now Lucifer saw that Abel would sleep with his sister Lith and a positive world will spring up and continued from that union and will cut off from their father Adam and mother Eve, she quickly assassinated Abel. This is just to cut-off that offspring. **I** also put the wandering spirit in Cain so that he would not sleep with Lith. Her idea was that with Abel dead, Cain would marry Lith. The incubator of Abel was to bring out the seeds of God. So, if Cain had slept with Lith, pollution would take place. With this original understanding and plan **I** quickly made him a mad person and the head of human-animals. Then **I** used the blood of Abel that went into the ground at Realm of Soul of Creation and created King Solomon and Queen Bathsheba, the mother of Solomon.

Of course the Father is Adam, which **I** passed through many generations from Abraham and then concluded with Abraham's appreciation to materialize King David. Through King David **I** then materialize King Solomon. Through King Solomon **I** materialized Joseph incarnate of David's transit to have a son who was his Father, back as Christ, the original Adam in the higherself. Our Lord Jesus Christ launched the new world, THE NEW CREATION. So through this the New World is now established.

Jesus Christ and Abel, who is King Solomon, have the same star. They are the TWINSELF of **THE FATHER GOD,** The Designer and the Word. Abel did not have any child but **I** use the spirit of Abel to identify all children of God, which is the Dove of God called the Holy Ghost. Abel's higherself who is our Lord Jesus Christ the higher soul and the higherself of his Father Adam and his higher soul of King Solomon came back on earth as our Lord Jesus Christ. He was a virgin just as Abel was. **I** use the Spirit that came out from Jesus Christ The Holy Spirit to inspire all children of THE FATHER GOD and identify all **THE FATHER GOD'S** children. Now we have **THE SUPREME FUTURE** through the Holy Spirit of truth, I **AM THE SUPREME FUTURE,**

THE HOLY SPIRIT OF TRUTH, THE THIRD UNIVERSAL SUPREME WORD PERSONIFIED ON EARTH, the first time **I** was personified as **ADAM**, the second time **I** personified as **OUR LORD JESUS THE CHRIST** and finally **I** personified as the **HOLY SPIRIT OF TRUTH, LEADER OLUMBA OLUMBA OBU**. That is the reason that if you do not baptise with the water and the spirit you will not be identified as a child of God. That is the essence of baptism. Previously circumcision was used, that is, to spill blood was the only means that was used for identification. When that was done, it is used to identify the children of Israel as the children of Abraham.

John the Baptist introduced another means by water when he

used baptism to identified **OUR LORD JESUS CHRIST** and through the identification of **OUR LORD JESUS CHRIST** came about the identification of all children of God through the Holy Spirit of truth today. So the water, the blood and the Spirit constitute the Trinity God. For this reason interaction should be done in positive manner. For your interactions you have to differentiate from the human-Gods and the Human-animals. You have to be very careful whom you interact with. If you sleep with animal you will soil your template. When you read the Lecture Revelation titled – 'THE DIVINE OFFSPRING' – you will get more information on this. There is also more in 'DIVINE SELF'.

THE FATHER'S TALK
Lectures Revelation take people

nearer and near to **THE FATHER GOD** through the Wide Angle of God, which covers the entire creation. Therefore, Wisdom and Understanding have now come together to promote the Will of **THE FATHER GOD**, and the Glory of THE **FATHER GOD** on earth. The lower part of Understanding is Clever, which is the spirit for Science and Technology that brings physical comfort to earth. The lower part of Wisdom is knowledge that will be used to materialize all this training to bring comfort to lives. So everything is united together – the spirit, water and blood and that are the system of the Divine God in human form.

THE FUTURE
A: **ARRANGEMENT**
B: **DIVINE LIFE**

Through all the information provided now you know that the future is established. **THE SUPREME FUTURE** is now established. **THE SUPREME FUTURE** that is establishing now is careful arrangement, official arrangement, and improvement of life, quality of life. It is not quality of life of physical amenities alone, but quality of positive spiritual life that includes peace, humility, mercy, oneness, and equality. All these things bring perfect quality of life. They bring peace for life. This is the present New World; the future Supreme New world that is coming now which **THE FATHER GOD** is setting up now. This is the template of the

New World. These entire templates now established today will control the entire universe and other planets. That is the reason **I** said that this Lecture Revelation – **THE SUPREME FUTURE** – is a companion for every soul. Everything is covered.

At the end of this Lecture Revelation attach 'THE BUDGET OF THE NEW WORLD' to it. So that everybody will know the Divine Emblem – the true identity that will form the complete companion for everybody.

Now, you can see that the Divine New World, which is the future itself, has been arranged as contained in this Lecture Revelation. The explanations cover the Natural life and the Spiritual life.

The Divine life of children of **THE FATHER GOD** is peace,

love and clean heart. You do not plan evil. You do not have anything to do with animal life. Love every creation but do not make friends with animals because when you make friends with animals you are interacting with them. As **I** already mentioned, that is the proof that you are human-animal.

Animals have no love for man. Animals have no peace. Animal is premature nature that has no instinct of schooling. They cannot learn how to love. However, when the animal improves and migrates and takes evolution to human then it can learn advanced life of love to become understandable and speak as human God. They are still low natures.

So, you who have already developed to be a human being should progress to SUPREME

FUTURE. From your past as human-animal and to elementary man you should now progress to love, which is cross, tolerance, peace and so on. Get more on this from the Lecture Revelation 'PRIMARY, SECONDARY AND UNIVERSITY OF BROTHERHOOD'. You should be progressing – moving forward. The Divine Life is when you become the Christ of God, Servant of God, one with THE FATHER GOD and work in the Christhood office. As **I** said, Christ means King and King means The Anointed. The Supreme Anointed Person is the one **I** call The King of Kings and The Lord of Lords that is Christ Himself **GOD THE FATHER**, The Anointed Spirit of **THE FATHER GOD**, THE UNIVERSAL SUPREME WORD.

When you take note of things like the trainings stipulated here, you are now short-listed and will be given assignments to understand **THE FATHER GOD.** You are short-listed as the first step of Brotherhood. When you are selected - you are selected to have courses and to take exams and have to pass the exams of love one another. When you pass the tests of love one another, you will then be elected into the office of Christ, as a Servant of Christ. With the practical Christianity of love one another, you are then appointed and sealed as a King. Under that Umbrella is the King of Kings as the Head of Christhood and then we have you as a Christ Servant – as a Servant of God – as one of the Kings.

That is the reason there is King of Kings and the Lord of Lords.

People have no understanding of this but through this **SUPREME FUTURE** you will know.

Kings must be Servants of the Lord Most High and will be the people that passed and have at least positive five good stars, which include mercy, love righteousness, kindness, peace and the rest of other God's characteristics. You have to bear the twelve fruits of THE HOLY SPIRIT OF GOD. It is not easy to bear fruit of TRUTH and you cannot get it for free or bribe, the only way through is have the total LOVE of THE FATHER GOD. It is not a political thing.

People believe that they can jump the queue from human-animal to Christ. No way! You must be Human-God first by evolution. When you become Human-God, you will take the first, second, third until the seventh stages of Brotherhood, not what you called white, black and so brotherhood, I mean BROTHERHOOD of **THE FATHER GOD ALMIGHTY** and practice love for one another as Christ did. Carry your own burden. When you are forgiven and you paid all the debts you will be promoted to Christ Office. You will thereafter become free in your soul. Your assigned star will then be waiting for you, which is the Holy Spirit; by this point you gain back your lost soul in the BROTHERHOOD of STAR with **ME THE FATHER GOD** through **MY** Divine Self, **THE HELPER, THE** HOLY SPIRIT of TRUTH, and **THE COMFORTER of MANKIND**. From the training of understanding and love you then attract the Holy Spirit to yourself that will automatically give you the Star. Now you become the Peace of God - one with **THE FATHER GOD.**

When you are in the star that is when you have Divine Love and you are truly a member of the Future World - THE SUPREME NEW WORLD, **THE SUPREME FUTURE**. With this you become one of the Gods of the earth. Like **FATHER** like **SON**. Anything you speak stands. All spirits, all angels, and all demons – all the people you ran away from as you were progressing will bow down for you. There is no doubt about this as it is computerised system. You cannot bribe anybody or the angels to do this without coming from the spirit.

When Abel was promoted to the higher soul of Heaven every spirit bowed down for him. When he came back on earth as KING SOLOMON, the Angel Michael gave Him a Star of Power and that Energy of Power was called ***Subjection and Frustration*** to your ***CREATOR***. That Seal has been in Solomon spiritually since then and the same seal **I** give His Royal Majesty King Solomon David Jesse ETE today. That was the seal, which King Solomon used to control all demons and all spirits to bow down and they laboured for the building of the Temple of God. That Temple of God is the same establishment of the Kingdom of God today.

It is only your enemy that must bow at your feet. Who are those enemies? Remember **I** said in the Psalm of David, David stay at **MY** side until **I** make your enemies become your footstool. That

Psalm manifested through King Solomon when all demons bowed down for him and he used them to build the House of God. The same covenant **I** make today that those who love **ME, I and MY FATHER** will come and live with them. The same thing manifested in Christ and **I** came to live in HRM King Solomon David Jesse ETE now to talk, talk and talk for eternity. So, what is there to doubt about this whole thing?

Promises always come to fulfilment. The new covenant of God is love and since you love one another **I** live in you. Any human being that practices love and stop practicing negativism **I** will live with them. **I** will clean your environment and Divine Spirit will be with you and you will live Divine life of God.

C: MANIFESTATION OF WORLD PEACE

THE SUPREME FUTURE is to manifest the world peace. In the world of today are Politicians full of arrogance, strife, and envy and cunning. They steal and are armed with weapons then say they want to make peace in the world. How can you make peace in the world while you are not a peacemaker? Are you a peacemaker? If you are a peacemaker then you are a child of God. Apparently you are not as you are afraid that someone will kill you so when you go to make peace you carry gun. When the enemy sees you with gun, what do you think will happen? He will also carry gun and shout at you in the distance so that you would not craftily kill him.

Is this not the wisdom of the world, which Satan uses to

deceive people? You went to help a country, instead of offering the assistance you engage in a war with them. How can you believe such a story like that? Everybody should believe the truth. Nonetheless, this time around everyone's eyes are opened. Every nature has improved and nobody should follow another blindly anymore. If you follow blindly you will fall into the pit and before you discover you are being deceived it will be too late.

Do you know that people gang up in spirit to manipulate people's lives? They gang-up to know who you are. They gang-up to know your star. They gang-up to know how much you earn and they gang-up to control this world. They gang-up like that because you are not aware of what is going on. Nevertheless, since **I** have established **MYSELF** in you through the Wisdom of God, the gang-up of the world is destroyed. You will see that **I, THE FATHER GOD THE CREATOR OF THE UNIVERSE** will give peace to the whole world through individual peacemakers. If today you have made peace, peace will follow you.

ALL CITIZENS OF UNITED STATES OF AMERICA LISTEN TO THESE INSTRUCTIONS AND STOP GOING TO WAR AND MAKE PEACE FOR PEACE TO FOLLOW YOU.

IF THE UNITED KINGDOM WANTS PEACE, AND THEY TAKE IT AS THEIR DUTY TO GO TO MAKE PEACE WITHOUT WEAPONS, THEN PEACE WILL FOLLOW THEM.

All the weapons – bombs this, nuclear that, tornado and all the rest of the weapons, should be destroyed and recycled to produce aeroplanes for positive conveyance of people from one place to another. Or make fans – air coolants or build houses, anything good with them. There are millions of people out there looking for accommodation. You should build houses all over the world. Every child that is born today and indeed everyone in the whole world should be housed. There should be free houses for all. In addition to free accommodation, must be free electricity, free gas, free water and free transport. Such basic things should be free and sufficiently so for all mankind. Instead Satan uses the amenities of God for suppression. All the creations –

minerals, oil, diamond, gold and so on - all the things for good life are wasting away for nothing but arrogance, envy and strife and because of greediness. Big belle eats big food!

From today onwards nobody should *follow-follow* (follow others sheepishly or be misled) again to avoid falling into the pit of Hell fire.

D: **LIVE AND LET LIVE**

The World Peace is Live and Let live. It is a character. It is an attribute. It is an understanding. It is an agreement. Every soul from the belly, family member, compound, work place, community level, state level, office, relation, church – all should start now to live that life - the life of peace - live and let live

- mind your own business. If you adopt the life of live and let live, peace will start to establish where you are. Peace will not jump in from the air to establish anywhere. The peace will start from right your family.

If all the families in America practice live and let live and all the families in Iraq practice live and let live, including the entire Arab world there will be peace. If all the children of Abraham believe that they are all from the same father, even though different mother they will live in peace. Naturally the land that yields cocoyam may not be too good for planting yam. Equally, the land that is used to grow fruits may not be good enough to plant other crops. Every land is assigned different crops, but the same farmer owns them. Abraham had two different children. Isaac was a spiritual child because of the spiritual life of Abraham being human God on Earth – natural Father. The first son Ishmael was a physical child because Abraham was a warrior with remnant of animal blood from the time of Adam. He was a man of war to salvage his people. So these two children should come to an understanding now with this **SUPREME FUTURE** New World. That assignment of old is finished.

Esau and Jacob are of the same father and mother. Ishmael and Isaac are also of the same father. They should stop fighting and quarrelling. They should make peace and believe that they are one and mind their business as well. The blessings **I** gave to Isaac, he should keep it. The blessings **I** gave to Ishmael he should keep it also. Spiritual thing and carnal things should unite together for the sake of peace in the system of **THE SUPREME FUTURE**. If you are spiritual, you will take care of the spiritual kingdom as you hear or read these words. The carnal people also should use their money to support this wisdom. Therefore, with all uniting and working together there is peace. Do not turn back to say you are ruling this world. Who are ruling for? Who are you ruling with? Are you not of the same spirit, water and blood as others? So, with love, equality must reign. With love, peace must reign and that is Brotherhood of the same parent ADAM and EVE. That also is love. Whether you are a Christian, whether you are a Moslem, whether you are Judaism –

anything you are, Brotherhood entity of one father one mother must take reign in **THE SUPREME FUTURE NEW WORLD** in the Name of Our Lord Jesus Christ Amen.

E: **MARRIAGE, NEW OFFSPRING**

The reason **I** said Cain should not marry the wife of Abel was because he would have injected the template of vampire into the wife of Abel. When Abel came back as King Solomon he looked for his wife, but could not find her. That was the reason he said, 'blessed is the man who has found his wife'. He could not find his wife and if he had found his wife, he would have had a child that would have taken over his throne. Rehoboam was not his spiritual child, he was incarnate Absalom,

Absalom was incarnated Cain the brother of Abel. Rehoboam was not a son that came from Solomon's blood, but he was born by Solomon, what happen was that as soon Absalom die since he is family soul, he stand by and come back to take the first born position and rule with the evil spirit, that was why the kingdom end. The same things happen when King James lives the throne. You can have a child and the child is not directly from you maybe from other you know, you know. When you have a child that is from you, you will see that the child really inherited you in the correct life. Since King Solomon could not find his wife, he could not have heritage. However, Bathsheba was incarnate positive part of Eve and he Solomon was Abel, and David was the same natural Adam. It was also Abel's blood that **I** was used to create Bathsheba and so she was part of David. Therefore, when David met Bathsheba the connection was already there. The negative spirit that was around through the former husband organized the meeting. King Solomon thereafter received his father's inheritance because David produced the photocopy of his positive self as Solomon. So, any day that you marry someone who is your other half, you will not have problems, because you will have copy of the real you – *Amiso* of you and this is the meaning of marriage.

If you behave well with **THE SUPREME FUTURE** and Supreme understanding of **THE FATHER GOD'S** wisdom then you will make prearrangement for your future marriage. How do you make prearrangement for your future marriage? This is very important because marriage is continuation template maker. Woman and man are the makers of continuation template of human offspring. That aspect therefore, is very important.

Since you are in the School of Higherself Brotherhood Mastership and you understood that in the past you fornicated and committed adultery, engaged in prostitution, told lies and did all sorts of things printable and unprintable and in so doing created all sorts of energy around you. The bad energy now does not give you a good template and does not allow you to have a good thing. That is the past. You now have to work for the future.

When you work for the future, you correct the past here in the present by refraining from that life of old. Make a confession to your partner. If you are a man you would not hide the things you did and the woman too should not hide what she did. After the confession both of you should pray and take evolution away from that past. Then the blood of Christ, which is the remedy, the energy of improvement, the energy of promotion will promote you and give you the Holy Spirit. Holy Spirit now becomes your God Father – your Spiritual Father. When the Holy Spirit now becomes your Spiritual God Father, then **I, THE FATHER GOD ALMIGHTY, THE SUPREME NATURE** with **MY** Super Holy Spirit in **ME** will create a new template for you. When **I** create the new template for you with good character and good life, your future is supreme though for sometime you will still carry small, small problems and small, small crosses in present life. When you finished then your future becomes supreme. That is when you will have **SUPREME FUTURE** – good life and your child. The offspring you will have will not bring your past influences back again. Your influence will be from the present, which you will reproduce in the future. That is how to create a new future. This is for the serious minded people that want to help the nature, which is God and help this world to be a perfect new world to come in future. Of course there is no pressure.

If you are not a member of this program you will not surface again here on earth. If however, you happen to be born into this earth plane by accident **I** will assign you to human-animal to leave in the bush.

F: **ONE WORLD AND UNIVERSAL IDEOLOGY**

This is the idea of one world and universal ideology. When you say one world, it is unity of all God's creation with **THE FATHER GOD.** One world ideology will now be **FATHER GOD, FATHER GOD, FATHER GOD, and FATHER GOD ALMIGHTY** with all **MY** positives creations. What **I** mean by **FATHER GOD** is the **HOLY SPIRIT TRUTH, THE CREATOR OF THE UNIVERSE.**
FATHER GOD, FATHER GOD, FATHER GOD is the original understanding that Our

Lord Jesus Christ brought to the earth. Through the name of our Lord Jesus Christ, **THE FATHER GOD** has now established **HIMSELF** as the owner of the whole universe. **HE** is **THE SUPREME OWNER, THE RIGHTFUL OWNER.** Every creation so long as you surrender and recognize the existence of **THE FATHER GOD** all is well with you. That becomes the wonderful ideology of the new world – **THE SUPREME FUTURE OF THE FATHER GOD,** because Christ has paved the way. Everywhere is Christ, Christ, Christ and **THE FATHER GOD**, Children of **THE FATHER GOD** in diverse forms. It does not matter the name of the organization you belong to, but since you become a Christ servant of **THE FATHER GOD** in the **UNIVERSAL BROTHERHOOD** of the same **UNIVERSAL PARENTHOOD** and you believe in Christ you are forward – the future. It is under that Christhood alone – mind you that Christ does not mean *owo* or human. Christ as **I** explained is in charge of the Moslems. HE is in charge of Judaism. HE is in charge of Christians. HE is in charge of all creations. Christ means the king of Kings and the Lord of Lords, The Word, The Spoken Word, the Owner, the Proprietor, the Converting Energy – all mean Christ, the King. It is a language. You can tell somebody and people that Christ means, the anointed, it is stamp. The only stamp that when it is applied on somebody it is approved, using the physical situation as analogy - you appended your signature and collected money from the bank and no one questioned your withdrawal, because the owner of the cheque signed blank cheque for you to withdraw whatever amount you wanted. That is Christ. If you want to worship **THE FATHER GOD**, Christ is the one to sign for you to do that. Which God are you worshipping? If you worship the one that Christ sanctioned that is the original God. That is the real God.

That is the reason **I** said that **I** HAVE CONQUERED THE LAST TEMPTATION ON THIS PLANET WHICH WAS AN ATTEMPT TO REMOVE THE NAME OF OUR LORD JESUS CHRIST AWAY FROM BROTHERHOOD OF THE CROSS AND STAR.

Since **I** have conquered that and **I** put the name of our Lord Jesus

Christ, the blood of our Lord Jesus Christ in everything that obtains in Brotherhood of the Cross and Star. That is the gateway and that is the Sole Spiritual Head. **HE IS THE FATHER** and **HE** is one with The Son. **I stand at the gate.** Where will you pass from to get through? You have rubbish intent. You do not want to pass through Christ to avoid being x-rayed then you are doing rubbish. Christ means x-ray. Christ means the Spirit that is in charge. You cannot override your manage and issue your own instructions. In the light of that, before you speak and before you do anything, you must, **I** repeat and emphasize that you must pass through the name of our Lord Jesus Christ. If you do not do that then you are rebel. Now back to the point.

Everything has become **FATHER GOD, FATHER GOD, FATHER GOD** the Blessed New World, the divine peace, the ideology of every creation and even including animals, birds and fishes. Every mind is **FATHER GOD, FATHER GOD, FATHER GOD;** Peace, Peace, Peace- one world and Universal ideology, one entity, one unity, love, love, love. That is the New Covenant ruling the whole world. That is the reason **I AM** giving this Lecture Revelation today. This is the week that King Solomon celebrates yearly the Covenant of the New World and Universal – Love, Love, and Love that will stay for eternity and has everything to do with the Supreme New World.

G: **THE UNIVERSAL GOD**

The universal God is love. Talking about **THE FATHER GOD** is universal **LOVE, THE UNIVERSAL WORD OF CREATION**, which is GOD. When you talk about the Son, you are referring to the Universal God. Universal God is love. It is the Christ of God, the Son of God. HE is **THE UNIVERSAL SUPREME WORD**. HE is love. HE is the Universal God. There is no other God than Love. It is said – blessed are the peacemakers for they shall be called the children of God. Blessed are the pure in heart for they shall see God. In that respect, if you are called Jehovah God and you are not clean in heart, how the name Jehovah sounds in the ear of people that sees you become abomination. If, in the name of God you call yourself Holy Spirit or you call yourself Jehovah or Emmanuel, matter of fact, any name you call how it will sound correct even as you are living wicked life. People will nevertheless, observe your life and notice that your life is not a positive one and that the fruit you bear does not portray your representations. Conclusively, you are a deceiver and a false prophet and people will regard you as such. Therefore, it is not the name and it is not the title, but the spirit that counts. It is the fruit of the Holy Spirit truth ideology – one world and universal oneness with **THE FATHER GOD**, one peace, love, and humility, including promotion of every good thing, lover of every good thing that matters. If you see somebody that you know that have **THE FATHER GOD'S** Holy Spirit truth you should love that person, you should corporate with that person and interact with the person. Most of you don't do that. You'd rather associate and interact with armed robbers, fornicators and adulterers. You go with those that fly - mostly at night, because you do as they do. Birds of the same feather fly together.

If therefore, you are a righteous person and if you are a peaceful person you should always mingle with people of like characters. If you are somebody that loves **THE FATHER GOD,** you will know the persons that love **THE FATHER GOD** also and you will mingle with such persons.

Gangs have sprung up everywhere. All the evil people have put themselves in gangs. **I** have grouped them in spirit by nature. Nature does not take bribe. It does not take rubbish. Whatever behaviour you portray, nature puts you in your group. Any group you find yourself know that, that is what you are. If you do not find yourself in any group know that your group members are not yet come and you are a group yourself.

Say, you are a peaceful person and you've looked around and cannot find any peaceful person, stay by yourself with **THE FATHER GOD.** When your group comes you will see them. Do not force yourself and say – I cannot stay alone. I have to mingle with people. If you mingle you will soil your template and have failed in this **Future Supreme New World and universal LOVE ideology**. So be careful and be in spirit. Be with **THE FATHER GOD** and **THE FATHER GOD'S** Holy

Spirit will always be directing you.

F: **SOCIAL AMENITIES**

The social amenities are the gifts of God. **I** give light free; good health free; the sun free; rain is free; air is free, blood **I** give free, water is free, life free – everything **I** created **I** give you free. You walk on this ground free. However, the enemies of **GOD THE FATHER** – those **I** call enemies are those who formulate laws to charge for air, electricity, water – they charge for everything. So much so you cannot even put anything in the air. Now there is no availability of free radio station anymore because you must get license from - whom? You must obtain license from someone or somewhere before you communicate.

Communication is a free wave; it is the wave that caused communication to work. Somebody has a way to communicate with one another, but another person sat somewhere and calls himself 'big-man' in this world and formulates law so that they can give licence to their companion, their fellow evil people thereby making lives difficult for people. Don't you see that telephone calls from Britain to America and Australia cost next to nothing -one penny, sometimes it is free, but to call some others poor countries like African countries you pay through your nose? Yet these are the people they should help the most. Why don't you give African countries free telephone for say five, ten years or so until they get up from the ground, if you really love people?

I know the tricks and what they are all up to in this world. They have polluted the world and Satan incarnates are bent on duping innocent people. That is the reason **I** brought out **THE SUPREME FUTURE** doctrine for the whole universe. Any President, any Prime Minister, any King, any Queen, any Church Leader and any other leaders and all prominent people and official persons and what have you, if you love your self as a positive human being with the love of **THE FATHER GOD** in you make life easy for all and give free amenities to everybody on earth. You are a Preacher, you are a Minister, if you want to make money, think over it first in relation to **THE FATHER GOD** and all the creations of God including the human beings. To make life equal give free amenities to them. Social amenities of God let lives have equal living. First and foremost, when a child is born steps must take to provide for these basic needs in life free. They need accommodation – free accommodation, free food, free water, free electricity and free telephone. The basic amenity every human being must be provided for free is inclusive of transport. Thereafter, if the person wants to live big they can do so and provide the luxury for themselves, but five free amenities must be provided free for citizen of the earth. These include accommodation, water, electricity, communication and feeding, the general one is a universal network road. All of those things that make life easy should be free.

Every government of the whole world should come together – if you call yourself world power and that you are working for **ME THE FATHER GOD**, this is the book for you. You must read this Lecture Revelation. It does not matter if you have twelve horns, one hundred horns or big seven heads. You are not bigger than SUPREME NATURE. You must go to six feet under the ground one day. Do you not pass out wastes – excrement and all?

I want to reveal that there is an errand no one can send anybody. No friend can send a friend to do such things for each other or for one another. No lover can send a lover. No one can go to the toilet and defecate or urinate for you. Call it any fancy name or make any fancy reference you wish - little room, powder room, lavatory, ladies, gents, gentlemen, cloakroom, spend a penny - whatever. Your lover, husband, wife, child or anyone for that matter cannot expel faeces from yourself for you. Queen or King– of any land, President or Prime Minister, Heads of State, or any ruler cannot say to anybody take a seat inside me and pass out the faeces for me. You have to do these things by yourself.

Your toilet is therefore your burial ground. By the time you finished with going through this teachings, you must have visited the lavatory, before, after or during. You sleep also. Don't you? If you pass out waste and if you sleep also that means you are not more powerful than **THE FATHER GOD.** It means your power is not greater than death and burial ground. Therefore, humble yourself before THE FATHER GOD ALMIGHTY and take instructions for the Glory of THE FATHER GOD to manifest. Do not fight against **ME** any more on this earth just because **I** kept quiet.

Where you refuse to listen **I** will render you so incapacitated that you cannot clean your bottom by yourself after visiting the lavatory. Or **I** send you to the burial ground where you will never come up. That is what will happen. **I** have been doing that to all the people that claim that they are Gods on earth, practices evils and wickedness on a fellow human beings. You do not hear of these people any more. Even those who claimed they killed Jesus Christ, where are they today? All the countries of the world that claim to represent God and doing wicked, where are they? America is supposed to be a Missionary country. Britain was made the home base for Missionaries, but they deviated from that ordinance. When **I** sent King Solomon to incarnate as King James to come and establish the United Kingdom, it was because **I** wanted the United Kingdom to be the home to spread the word of God and the Doctrine of Christ and he established it. However, due to the bad seeds in the Monarchy the doctrine was spoilt and the bad seed spread all over. Then **I** led them to America and they established United States of America.

In the United States of America the evil spirit followed suit – again, and established it headquarters in California and

spread from there and polluted the doctrine. That brought all sorts of problems to America – trouble upon trouble and still on going. However, Britain and America still have the chance to repent. When they repent, their governments will start positive charity and not charity by politics. It is not the charity that you caused the problems – in disguise and then provided the solution. You make someone to be ill so that they attend your hospital. You instigate someone to fight so that you send weapons and pretentious assistance as aid. You look for trouble in a bid to utilize your nuclear weapons and then turn around and provide charity to the people you destroyed. No! That is wrong charity! That is evil!
I established an original charity through King James and the

United Kingdom was to salvage the whole world and make them one in peace and become the home. If you have problems in your place you come and stay here until your problem is over then they sent you back. That system of policy – the ***Democracy*** of **THE FATHER GOD'S LOVE** was established for good courses. It is not this your current democracy to demonstrate evil. The Democracy of God established, was to demonstrate love, oneness with all creations in the physical manner. That is what is called charity. They rather turned charity to something else. They trapped banks, all sorts of people and things and use the money and all to sponsor evil and evil spread all over the world. **MY SOUL** is not happy with all these things!

Therefore, from this day every member of this world who wants to and share with **THE SUPREME FUTURE WORLD** must hearken to **ME** and stop their actions of past events and use the present to correct past events for a better future, in the name of our Lord Jesus Christ. Amen.

When you practice love for one another and when you have become one and the spirit of oneness reigns, the good amenities of God will then spread all over the world. There are some places in this world today that still so backward and so walk about naked. There are places that still kill twins. There are so many traditions still operating in this world that do not bring glory to **ME THE FATHER GOD ALMIGHTY THE CREATOR OF THE UNIVERSE**. That was

MY reason of establishing the United Kingdom to go all over the world and destroy those traditions in peaceful manner.

Let the peace of God rule in Brotherhood of the same parent with Supreme Star of the Holy Spirit of Truth so that everybody – wherever you are, practice love for one another. Human beings do not rule the world. The Holy Spirit HIMSELF from today till eternity, in the name of our Lord Jesus Christ, rules the world. Amen.

G: **THE TRUE SERVANTS**

The True Servants of **THE FATHER GOD ALMIGHTY** are the people that will carry this message to all human beings. They must promote this message through any and all the means available - by cash, sponsorships, media, the internet, air, news, books and others.

The True Servants of God must sponsor **THE SUPREME FUTURE** instructions to the whole world so that everybody should have access to it. Anybody who undertakes it upon himself or herself to spread this good news has become a Servant of the Lord. **I AM** using the mouth of His Royal Majesty Senior Christ Servant, King Solomon David Jesse ETE to deliver this Lecture Revelation from the Archives Record of Original King Solomon Spiritual Library of **THE FATHER GOD** from the time of **ABEL.** Since **I** have done this as well as with other information, if you promote them you are directly a positive servant of **THE FATHER GOD**. Also a Servant of God will assist in prayers and psalms and songs to allow the will of God to materialize.

All Kings and Queens are servants of **THE FATHER GOD**. All Presidents and Prime Ministers are servants of **THE FATHER GOD**. All Heads of Churches and Armies, Community leaders, all youths – everybody is a Servant of **THE FATHER GOD**. Spread the news of **THE SUPREME FUTURE, THE SUPREME NEW WORLD** to all children. Even your child you have just given birth to, teach them the Doctrine of **THE SUPREME FUTURE,** the doctrine of the new word of **THE FATHER GOD** and not the new world order they are parading about. There is no new order anything other than to love one another; other than **THE FATHER GOD, THE HOLY SPIRIT OF TRUTH.** It is the

Brotherhood of the same **FATHER GOD** and the same **MOTHER GOD,** which has come to stay and with love for one another and that will bring the perfect New World, which is Star. That is the reason for the name **BROTHERHOOD of the CROSS and STAR** – the Past, Present and the Future, respectively. The future is everlasting life.

H: **EVERYTHING IS FATHER GOD, FATHER GOD, FATHER GOD**

Everything from this point will become and has become and shall be **FATHER GOD, FATHER GOD, and FATHER GOD. FATHER GOD** here, **THE FATHER GOD** there and **FATHER GOD** Universal this, **FATHER GOD** Universal that. **I** established World Bank for the children of God called Olumba Universal Charity World Bank Account and the original King Solomon who has the directives on how to operate equality with humanity manages that Bank through THE UNIVERSAL SUPREME WORD SEASON CELEBRATION. Therefore, every government, every state, every family, homes, local governments, communities, churches, organisations, all factions, groups, clubs and sections, indeed the entire world must contribute a charity path to **ME** in appreciating the **FATHER GOD**. This is not a tithe and freewill offerings but a charity. The charity aspect will go to **FATHER GOD** Universal Charity World Bank Account, God Present.

I, THE SOLE SPIRITUAL HEAD THE SUPREME WORD OF THE UNIVERSE have decreed this and **I, THE SPIRIT OF THE SUPREME FATHER, THE HOLY SPIRIT OF TRUTH** have decreed this again, that the whole world shall put their income in this program. Any Human-God, any human soul or anybody that supports this by contributing one kobo or one penny will have a return blessing of over one million kobo or penny as the case may be. Also maximum spiritual security and maximum spiritual insurance will follow you from the spirit **I** give to King Solomon of old and of now. In addition, if you want evil spirit to be frustrated before you - if you want demon to be frustrated before - if you want poverty to be frustrated before you and if you want any rubbish and anything unpleasant to be frustrated before you - the power that **I** give to King Solomon through **THE FATHER'S TALK (GOD PRESENT),** as **I** gave Him that power last time, **I** give Him again this time – that power will frustrate all those things for you. Support this program. When you support any of the **FATHER GOD** programmes King Solomon ETE is doing **I THE FATHER GOD THE HOLY SPIRIT OF TRUTH** will frustrate all the evil things, which are negative that frustrates you. It is only the Holy Spirit that will elevate you now and forever more. Amen!

CONCLUSION
A: DIVINE NATURE OF HUMAN BEINGS ON EARTH

This is the summarized part of this Lecture Revelation.
The Divine Nature of human being on earth starts right now. Since you have taken evolution to change over to good life, to peace, to mercy and to love, there is no more wars, no segregation, tribalism, no division, no strive and no envy. Practice love one another, kindness, righteousness and peace. All these good virtues have started the good nature of human being on earth.
Everybody that believes the contents of this Lecture Revelation and practice same, your offspring will start to yield good nature, good life and the world will be good automatically and with that

the true image and likeness of **THE FATHER GOD** is now established on earth, in the name of Our Lord Jesus Christ. Amen.

B: **NOT ONLY IN THIS WORLD BUT IN ALL PLANETS OF MANIFESTATION EXISTS THE FOLLOWING CHARACTERS**

What you have heard so far and what you still hear from this **SUPREME FUTURE** Lecture Revelation including the summaries will not only obtain here on this earth. This earth is a small universe – a small planet but the planet earth is very important because it is a visiting planet – a transit planet. Nevertheless, now **I** will make this planet a permanent home – resident home for the image and likeness of **THE FATHER GOD**.

In view of the fact that the image and likeness of **THE FATHER GOD** is created in this planet, **I** now keep this planet for the King of Kings, the head of all humans and angels to head all the planets including all the souls from the moon to the stars as well as all the terrestrial bodies. They all come here to take evolution for improvement and to have experience, as this earth is experimental home, experimental world, and a training ground.

To get to the destination requires to pass the first Brotherhood test and so on and so forth and unto the seven Brotherhood Stages to obtain the Brotherhood Degree, which is love one another and then to become a Master. The next step after Brotherhood Mastership is Higherself and to Christhood. At Christhood, you know you have to love one another. That love is where you emanated from - the Source and the Destination and that is **I THE FATHER GOD ALMIGHTY.**

Since you now know that the Source and Destination is **THE FATHER GOD** and it means love, you should love one another. That becomes the perfect new world and the soul of creation bears the improvement and love and the change extends to all planets.

Man can then go from this planet to another for an assignment and come back because you have to come back. I will now send the good souls to other planets even as you are here on earth. When you have love, when you have peace, when you have humility, when you believe **THE FATHER GOD,** when your environment is clean and you have clean heart, **I THE FATHER GOD,** the Spoken Word, the Holy Spirit in you, you being the house of **GOD**, I can take you to any planet to save a situation and bring you back immediately. You will now walk with **ME** everywhere, here and there, as **THE FATHER GOD PRESENT** is Everywhere, Here and There.

What is happening here is equally taking place in all other planets. **I** reproduce this Lecture Revelation, **The Supreme Future New World** to **Supreme New Planets, Supreme New Air, Supreme New Water, Supreme New Moon, Supreme New Star, Supreme New soul, Supreme New Terrestrials, Supreme New,**

New, and New. So that all the souls that will come to this world, come through the supreme future improvement energy and well arranged souls to help this planet, in the name of Our Lord Jesus Christ. Amen.

C: HUMAN FATHERS

The nature that improved and all the good things that would be happening in the **SUPREME FUTURE,** the Human Fathers will become Human Gods, Human peace, Human Love; peace God Father, love God Father, Mercy God Father, Humility God Father, faithful God father. All the human beings that will be men will become the God Fathers of all the good characteristics of THE FATHER GOD on earth. That also will be the same thing with the women – Good Mother, Good Children, Good Brother, Good Sister – all of them as you see in A, B, C, D…will be good, good, good formula of the good nature.

D: **FATHER AND MOTHER, CHILDREN, RELATIVES, RELATIONS**

Father and Mother, children, relatives and relations – all must be in good condition and good nature. As everybody has become one there are good relationships with everybody and one another. At the moment, because of the bad system a mother does not treat her child well and the children do not treat their parents well. Everything is scattered here and there. There is no unity anywhere. With the new world in contrast, everybody will become one.

Wouldn't it be a wonderful thing to see the parents, the children and everybody as one? They all corporate and no one will see anyone in evil way - as being a witch. None will see the other to be a prostitute or gossip, slanderer and all that and causing problems here and there. Since **THE FATHER GOD** has established the Blessed New World - The Supreme New World, **THE SUPREME FUTURE** is now established as *'I and My Father are One'*, Brothers and Sisters Incorporated in one love of **THE FATHER GOD**, of Christ, of Holy Spirit of Truth and will reign supreme in the whole world, in the Name of Our Lord Jesus Christ, Amen.

E: **ALL FRIENDSHIPS MUST BE WITH GOD, WITH FATHER AND MOTHER, BROTHER AND SISTER, POSITIVE HUMAN BEINGS IN GENERAL**

The Holy Spirit is a friendship entity to every one. The Holy Spirit is the feminine part of **THE FATHER GOD** that treats everybody very nicely and lovingly and blesses. He cooks, gets money for you, shops for you and basically does everything for you in spirit.

The Holy Spirit does everything for mankind, because He is the influence, the power, and the energy like electricity that does everything for man. The Holy Spirit is in charge of the friendship characteristics in God's manner. Just like when Abraham recognized God he became the friend of God.

With the friendship spirit positive friendship and behaviour between a mother and her children - her daughters and sons must prevail. There must be friendship between the father and his children – his sons and daughters; between daughters and sons; between husband and wife; between relations and between friends. Everybody must establish positive spirit of friendship relationship that is positive with one another. If you are positive and be a friend to someone who is not positive, they vomit their evil tendencies to you because friendship is closeness. Friend means understanding. Friend means trust. You trust your friend more than anybody else because that person is part of you. It is a voluntary acceptance of character into your character. A friend is not supposed to hide anything from his or her friend. Friends have no bad motives or no bad intentions. Therefore, this is the blessed powerful **Supreme Future** that is established with positive friendship spirit of oneness and unity in the whole universe Amen.

Let **MY** peace and blessing abide with entire world especially all positive children of **THE FATHER GOD** Amen

ENYE! ODUDU! ABASI MI! OOO! ZIM, ZIM, ZIM! ASSASU! POSITIVE! POSITIVE! POSITIVE!

In The Name Of Our Lord Jesus Christ In The Blood Of Our

Lord Jesus Christ Now And Forever More Amen!

THANK YOU FATHER.

Song:
In the beginning was the word and the word was God Allelu-u-u! - *Alleluia!* Allelu-u-u! - *Alleluia!* Allelu-u-u! - *Alleluia!* Through this Revelation Lecture all is well in the whole universe for eternity. Amen!

THANK YOU FATHER

Copyright © 2007 Kssl/hrmkingsdetteh All Rights are Reserved

KING SOLOMON SPIRITUAL LIBRARY

THE GOD ENCYCLOPAEDIA WORD OF INFINITY

FATHER'S TALK
(GOD PRESENT)

DATE: OA/OD/BOOD (FIRST APRIL TWO THOUSAND AND FOUR

THE SPIRITUAL BUDGET OF

THE SUPREME FUTURE & ABC OF WORD

BY THE SUPREME FATHER, THE CREATOR OF THE UNIVERSE

In the Name of Our Lord Jesus Christ, In the Blood of Our Lord Jesus Christ, Now and forever more

THE DIVINE BUDGET OF THE FATHER GOD FOR ALL HIS POSITIVE CHILDREN

Let **MY** peace and blessing abide and rest unto **MY** positive creation, through the name and the blood of our Lord Jesus the Christ.

The following declarations of **MY** budget are for the human Gods not for the human animals who refuse to believe the existence of **THE FATHER GOD, THE CREATOR OF THE UNIVERSE. I, THE FATHER THE CREATOR OF THE UNIVERSE** declare that from today, **I** have made everything new in spirit and in the soul and it is going to camera into the physical reality. That is why this budget has been created for the A of Peter Bood (first of April two thousand and four) the first month of the new world, and it is going to take effect on the A of Peter year BOOG, (two thousand and seven).

A,- Every creation including man, as the head should live in love and peace, unity, tolerance, with long patience, with one another.

B,- Every human God who sincerely believes **THE FATHER GOD THE CREATOR OF THE UNIVERSE** should completely and automatically stop believing in infidels of any kind and elementary spirits. Apart from worshiping the **SUPREME FATHER** and **HIS** Christ, nothing else is acceptable to worship.

C,- All of **THE FATHER'S** children, the human Gods should be aware of not speaking any negative word of any kind.

What comes from their mouth should be seasoned with salt and it should be the words of love and peace, understanding with one another.

D,- Charity practice- Share what you have in your position with one another. Exchange gifts with your fellow brethren.

E,- Forgiveness- Every human God, the positive children of **THE FATHER** should forgive one another so that **THE FATHER** will also forgive them.

F,- Be Merciful- Every human God, the children of The **HOLY FATHER, THE CREATOR OF THE UNIVERSE** should be merciful to one another so that they can obtain mercy for themselves.

G,- I have instructed all the angels in heaven and on earth to protect and guide all the positive divine children of **THE**

HOLY FATHER, the human Gods and nothing evil shall befall them.

H,- The Seal- All the chosen positive children of **THE FATHER** have been sealed on their foreheads, **THE FATHER'S** seal for their salvation and all principalities in heaven and on earth and in every realm knows and respects them.

I,- RESIGNATION FROM ANY SECRET SOCIETY.
All **MY** positive children should resign openly from any secret society or any secret cult by writing a letter to, His Holiness The King of Kings and The Lord of Lords Olumba Olumba Obu. The secret cults such as witchcraft practice in any form either white or black, having anything to do with the use of talisman, hanging or buried in any form, visiting a necromancer or a 'seer', consulting a native doctor for any form of help, hiding

to consult any evil man or herbalist for help of any kind and pretending to be **THE FATHERS** child. Using any means to see vision or healing, drinking, or putting things in your eye, or any other means of invocation. Whatever form of characteristic of worship should be ceased, apart from knocking head and doing full worship for **THE HOLY FATHER, THE CREATOR OF THE UNIVERSE,** you must confess openly by writing to His Holiness Olumba Olumba Obu before A of Peter BOOG, (first of April two thousand and seven).

AO,- Worshiping the Father in spirit and in truth-
Full worship of The **HOLY FATHER** must be observed by the true child of **THE FATHER** at all times. Knocking your head and observing humility of **THE FATHER'S** presence in you wherever you find yourself. First, you must say, in the name of our Lord Jesus The Christ, in

the blood of our Lord Jesus The Christ, now and forever more, Amen. Then OOO and confess your sin then, either you thank **THE FATHER** or thank **THE FATHER** and then present your request. All this means worshiping **THE FATHER** in spirit and in truth. You must do this with absolute faith and hope, and then give **THE FATHER** a few minutes of silent concentration then **THE FATHER** will communicate back with you.

AA,- Tithe, Free will offering and Charity- Tithe, free will offering and charity represent **THE FATHER**, Son and The Holy Spirit, The Trinity. AO % (ten percent) of tithe from individuals, family, company, village, town or city, community, local government or state, nation, belongs to **THE FATHER**. It stands for acceptance and absolute believe that **THE FATHER** is your **FATHER THE CREATOR OF THE UNIVERSE**

and it gives you protection, and that is the fruit of righteousness of all believers the human God, the offspring of the positive human God on earth. Tithe is **THE FATHERS** royal hood and it does not belong to anybody or any group of people. The way people are currently handling the tithe is not pleasing to **THE FATHER** so **I** have used this medium to correct it with love but after this well? No officer or any post holder in this Kingdom or in the world should have access to The Father's tithe. No second person or third party should even know the amount of tithe paid by individuals or groups of people apart from the individual or group of people who pay the tithe should know how much they have paid to The Father. With the exception of this, it is a fault and it is followed with a bad consequence.

It is only **MY** ambassador The Father's only representative The King of Kings and The Lord of Lords, The in charge of The

Leaders Office seat that has the right to know individual or group tithe payment. He is the one that signs for **THE FATHER.** No tithe should be kept in any way. When the tithe has not reached him physically, **I** cannot reply. That is the mistake people make; no tithe should pass through any transit. If you put any tithe in a tithe box in the house or in the Bethel, it should be transferred straight to **THE FATHER'S** Leader Office, but it is the day the tithe reaches **THE FATHER** through King of Kings, that is when you have paid your tithe. Individual or group of people should not borrow money to pay tithe. Do not pay tithe from your capital if you are a businessman, you pay tithe from anything that you earn from **THE FATHER**. You pay your tithe from your gain, your own money and not borrowed money. Do not pay tithe according to a vision given for a particular amount. Tithe is paid from your heart when you believe **THE FATHER** to be your God and

FATHER. Do not tell unbelievers to pay tithe to **THE FATHER.** Do **I** want tithe from unbelievers, those who do not believe me? Thou shall not teach thy neighbor to know God. Do you tell a child how to look after his parents?

Freewill offering- Free will offering is righteousness according to your ability and your love; you spread your hand for the purpose of building the Kingdom. You can donate your house, your land or your child, anything of anything to promote and build the kingdom and that is what The King of Kings and The Lord of Lords will be using to minister in the Kingdom by building and expanding the Kingdom in building of bethels, looking after full time workers and anything that will positive growth in the Kingdom. That is what will be used from believers not unbelievers. **I AM** not interested in donations from unbelievers.

Charity- Charity is to help one another in love that is the main practice of this Kingdom of God. Charity means love in a practical form - Donation of cash and kind. Olumba Universal Charity is based on this operation of charity donation in the universal way. Every human being on earth be it human God or human animal are entitled to benefit from this charity. **I** have revealed to Senior Christ Servant, King Solomon Etteh, that charity work is the greatest of this Kingdom. It is to look after the poor and the needy, the widows the orphans and the destitute and to relieve the poverty among humanity. Establish roads, electricity, and market for those who do not have and to make life easy and enjoyable for all humanity. King Solomon David Etteh is the director of this program. **I** make King Solomon David ETE the minister of charity universally, working for The King of Kings and The Lord of Lords looking after the poor saints, all missionaries and servants of

God, those who do not work. Helping all the refuge centers all over the world, in the time of problem and reconstruction, Charity is to show mercy to individuals and groups of people so that **THE FATHER GOD** will show mercy unto you. Our Lord Jesus the Christ is the head of mercy as our Lord Jesus Christ showed mercy onto mankind. Among the ten commandants, charity is the greatest.

Song:
Mercy and love, righteousness, kindness and peace signify brotherhood.

The star of Brotherhood- Mercy, love, righteousness, kindness and peace are the E (five) points of the star in Brotherhood. Mercy, love righteousness, kindness and peace represent the five right hand fingers of **THE HOLY FATHER**, the five points of a star for absolute blessing. That is the secret of the star. The true children of God have mercy and love and that is the star.

The star bearers of this Kingdom not cross bearers; this is the sign of star bearers.

AB, The blessing and reward- I have pronounced 'the blessing absolute' for all **MY** faithful children. From now onwards, all angels, spirits and man, should obey the children of God. No evil shall befall them. No death, no sickness, no poverty, no bad luck, no lack, no lamentation, you plant in time you reap in time. You plant small you reap plentiful. **I** have opened the window of love and pour dews of blessings for all **MY** positive children. **I** hear them when they call **ME**, **I** grant all their request in time, **I** take sorrow and stress away from them, **I** guide their soul against destruction, **I** remain their **FATHER** and they remain **MY** children and **I** will be merciful unto their sins and their sins, **I** will remember no more. **I** bless their seed and all their offspring. There is peace in the house, there is peace outside wherever they are there is peace.

Before now, now, and after now, there is peace. Everywhere, here and there, there is peace for them. Their souls are secured. I ban all evil operation against them. Any evil man or spirit that plans any evil operation against **MY** children **I** recall them back to the HOLE and they shall cease to exist.

Special blessings go to all the workers of God, the preachers, the spirited, those who take the gospel of **THE FATHER** to the world, baptizing people, **I** bless you in cash and kind and for any contribution to this Kingdom before now and now, **I** bless you this time and the time to come, the blessing is for you.

Individual general judgment (for conscience sake)-

In individual general judgment is your conscience. As **I** revealed to Senior Christ Servant King Solomon David Etteh, that from the A St Labbaeus Thaddeus BOOA (first January two thousand and one) every body reaps what they sow. If you even plan to kill you will be killed. I will not wait until you kill. I have the three steps against evil plan.

First when you conceive evil thought in your heart against anybody or even yourself I send the police number A (one) called 'Pricina'. He will monitor you for BD (twenty four) hours for your next step of action then if your next step is to confirm your plan to carry on, then the angel police Pricina will arrest you and hand you over to an angel called 'Harascina' who is number B (two) then you will be in the house of arrest, temporal prison to change your mind. If you do not change your mind or repent then the Harascina police will hand you over to the 'Ashdustcina', the police angel C (three). The angel of the messenger of death (transfer to the HOLE) then they will hand you over to the angel of destruction and they will put you in the waste bin and take you back to the HOLE and you cease to exist.

That is how **I** will eradicate all the evil on this earth so that people will live peacefully on this earth. So who ever that wants to avoid this doom should confess openly to who ever you have made the evil plan against and repent and make peace. No evil shall exist in this world. **I** have made provision for everything in this world.

Law of The New Covenant-The only law is the law of Christ. Love one another as Christ love you. **I** have promoted this law of Christ to the law of karma, which is the power of **MY** judgment under individual judgment of consciousness, the individual's general conscience. If unconsciously you make a mistake and something happens to someone you can be forgiven by pleading to **THE FATHER**

for forgiveness, but that will mean that you also forgive one another. If you deliberately plan evil against someone and then say that after that **THE FATHER** will forgive you **I** will not forgive you. You must forgive one anther before **THE FATHER** will also forgive you, therefore you reap what you sow. (Refer to the Everlasting Gospel index volume A (one) chapter BC (twenty three).

ANIMAL, FISH AND OTHER CREEPING THINGS-

The animals, the birds and all other creations have equal right to exist and for that reason nobody should kill them for any purpose. But if there is any wicked or evil animal they shall also reap their judgment. If they kill they shall be killed and if they stink, they shall be punished. They reap what they sow; even the big fish that eats other fish shall die. Every four living creatures including man should be a vegetarian and not consume life.

TREES AND GRASS-

Cutting and weeding of grass for a divine purpose is permitted such as plantation or tidying the place for beauty and using the tree for building and for good purposes that glorify The Father for the elevation and happiness of mankind. Any use for a positive purpose is permitted but any negative use such making drugs and making lethal weapons that destroy life is not permitted and the, users shall be judged. Before using any of the above for a positive reason you must seek permission from **THE FATHER** because they are 'co- existing creation of life'.

THE EARTH, SAND OR SOIL RESPECTIVELY-

The earth is full with all types of minerals like gold, silver, diamonds, aluminum, salt, lime stone, cement, crude oil, which gives petrol and kerosene etc, etc. Anybody that exploits any of these things, be it an individual, company or government, shall allocate AO% (ten %) to **ME** as the rightful owner and The Creator of these minerals. And anybody that exploits these minerals should be a promoter of Olumba Universal Charity and should sponsor and donate free will offering to promote the Kingdom and **THE FATHER'S** business. If any group, individual or company or government refuses to do this, they will face judgment and **THE FATHER** will send those C (three) angels to arrest them from the scene and they shall be sent to the HOLE and they shall cease to exist.

I send fire, **I** send rain, **I** send thunder and any thing that **I** have against the thief who exploits this minerals without the permission of The Owner, **ME**. If they do not believe this order they will believe. Nobody is permitted to dig the ground without positive use of the sand or the hole that they are digging, the earth, the sand and the soil respectively. The earth represents the **MOTHER GOD** and the sand or soil represent the body of Christ and its purpose is to produce food of all types to sustain man as the house for **THE FATHER**, the blood of Abel was this security of all the MINERALS AND WEALTH ON EARTH. It is only, *Senior Brother Abel, the incarnate King Solomon that has 'The Key, the Permission and Power to exploit them spiritually and in truth*.

We walk on the earth, the sand and soil, which are the Mother God and the Body of Christ so that we may have life. Nobody is permitted to bury anything in the ground apart from positive eatable seeds that bear positive food for man. Nobody is permitted to put any charm or concoction or any form of ritual sacrifice in the ground, if you do this you shall be arrested by the said angels above. You can eliminate fesses and it goes back to the soil in the arranged way, you can bury the corpse in the ground because these are the things that come from the soil originally. The food eaten by man is from the soil and when it comes out as fesses it can go back to the soil, man is created from the soil therefore when he dies he can go back to the soil. Anything that is from the soil can go back to the soil.

WATER- The water also represents Christ and **MY** spirit is on top of the water that generates life to human beings and all living organisms. Nobody is permitted to throw any waste such as corpse or to defecate or throw fesses or put chemicals or any waste product into the water. Throwing anything in the water in the form of sacrifice or ritual, worshiping of mermaid or juju or any form of incantation in the water is not permitted any more. The fish and other living organisms in the water should be left to live in comfort as man live on earth in comfort. Nobody is permitted to go fishing for food or for any other purpose and the fish is not permitted to eat other fish, they have what to eat, if they do this they shall face judgment and they shall be arrested by the said angels and shall be sent back to the HOLE and shall cease to exist.

FIRE-Fire is the energy of **THE FATHER** representing **THE FATHER, THE CREATOR OF THE UNIVERSE** as **HIS** anger. **I** create fire for many purposes. The first is positive. It is to heat to produce cold, to form the dew, to bless the peace of the land. This is controlled by the supreme energy of the sun. Did anybody know that **I AM** fire **MYSELF?** And **I** protect and safeguard the positive ones but the negative ones **I** consume. Nobody is permitted to burn anything negative in the form of rituals, juju practice or concoctions. The fire will consume those who do that and they will be returned to the HOLE and they will cease to exist. **I** have instructed the fire part of **MYSELF,** that any creation including human kind, who use blood to make money or to build, to construct or to acquire wealth or instigate any practice that is negative which does not bring glory to **ME**, it should consume within a second and we would not see them any more. It is only those who fear God and accept the good purposes of **THE FATHER** that will remain and the Fire shall not burn them. So everybody should know that **I AM** Fire, which consumes all manner of evil.

AIR- Air is **THE FATHER**, the oxygen, the producer of hydrogen and nitrogen. Every living organism has life through the Air that is generated by **THE FATHER, THE CREATOR OF THE UNIVERSE**. The Air is the most divine product of **THE FATHER**. Everything that breathes the Air should live a meaningful life, the life that benefits others, the positive life without negativism, and to fear and reverence, and to give respect to the Air itself, and the Generator of the Air, which is **THE FATHER**. This is life itself controlled by the power of the Spoken Word. Nobody is permitted to speak a negative word **or** breathe the Air and waste the time to do rubbish, something negative and evil of any form on this earth. It has come to the point that **I** have to reveal **MYSELF** as The Everlasting Supreme Oxygen Of Life, **The Spirit AIR**. Did anybody know that when you breathe the Air you are breathing **THE FATHER** into your system as the supreme energy of life? So for those who say that there is nothing like **THE FATHER GOD** that should be the end of that stupidity and nonsense. Did **I** or have **I** ever charged for the cost of Air? Can anyone pay? No one can pay and for this reason everyone, should worship, glorify, knock head, do everything to praise, sing, dance to glorify **ME,** absolutely **ME** only! Exception of this, **I** will cease the Air from you and the angels shall arrest you and you shall be sent to the HOLE and shall cease to exist for eternity! The Air is the cyclone and the hurricane and all these are part of **ME, THE SUPREME FATHER**, which **I** use to destroy anything, individual, city or town that do not give glory to **ME**. Can anybody or any government stand that?

SACRIFICE TO GOD-The sacrifice that is acceptable to **ME, THE FATHER GOD, THE CREATOR OF THE UNIVERSE** is as follows: To love **THE FATHER** in all thy heart, in all thy mind and in all thy soul, and to love your fellow human beings, and to forgive everybody and not count sin for any body, and to be prayerful, and testify about the goodness of **THE FATHER**. You must testify about all what **THE FATHER** has being doing for you, **HIS** beauty, and creation of the universe, and to sing praises all the time to glorify **MY** name, to form the melody in your heart, that is the sacrifice that will unite **MY** spirit and your soul together as your **FATHER GOD ALMIGHTY**. Also feasting for brethren which should not contain any life, it shall only consist of fruits, vegetables, seeds, biscuits, bread and Soya products in different forms, water and pure natural juices from fruits or vegetables. To communion with your fellow brethren is the only sacrifice that **I** want. Anything like going to the forest, river, the sea, mountain or anywhere and do anything in the form of worship or sacrifice has nothing to do with **ME.**

COMMUNICATION - The divine way of communicating with **THE FATHER** is through the following directives: by saying, In the name of our Lord Jesus Christ, in the blood of our Lord Jesus Christ, now and forever more Amen. You should knock your head, to communicate with **THE FATHER**. You fast and knock head and communicate with **THE FATHER**. When you knock head if you know that you are guilty in your heart for any reason you confess your sin to **THE FATHER**. After the confession of your sin you can talk to **THE FATHER** as you will talk to your physical Father or to your husband or your sister etc. **THE FATHER** is the Supreme Spirit of creation and is the supreme studio with a super transmission wave built inside you, so if you breathe the air and the oxygen that generates the system and that gives you the imagination to communicate. That is what **I** give to man. **I** have not given animals and other creation the communicative system with **ME, THE FATHER, THE CREATOR OF THE UNIVERSE,** which is called DECROMATICIAN. **I** gave creations communication instinct, which is called CROMAMOVE. They can only communicate through their instinct but they cannot communicate with **THE FATHER**, which is why they are elementary. Even human animals cannot communicate with God, **THE FATHER**, they are elementary creations. They do not have the super radio communication station of God. They are developing from animals but human Gods were created by **THE FATHER** as the image and the likeness of God that is why they have love, because God is love. The true children of God cannot kill or harm anybody. If you have the spirit of **THE FATHER** and the radio station is on, if any evil thought comes, **THE FATHER** stops it, and you say, *God forbid bad thing*, but the human animal do not have the transmitted communication from **THE FATHER** to stop them therefore they execute the evil that they think about, and that is the difference between human animal and human God.

BUSINESS AND ESTABLISHMENT FOR CHILDREN OF GOD- The following are the approved trades, businesses and establishments for children of God. Trading with any product that does not damage the character and the peace of human life is permissible. However, anything that damages and disturbs human life such as selling of tobacco and alcohol is not permitted. Trading of the human body in any form such as prostitution is not permitted. Trading of any type of weapon for killing or to manufacture or deal in them is not permitted for any child of God. Drugs and any such products that can be harmful to humans are not permitted to be traded by children of God. Anything that makes man uncomfortable or harms life in anyway is not permitted, such as guns, bombs, cigarettes, drugs and chemicals are not permitted.

Bars and clubs, hotels or brothels are not permitted, but guesthouses for positive reasons such tourism, accommodating ministry workers is permitted. Farming is permitted, but not to plant anything that will bring damage to human beings such as Tobago plants or any negative plant that is connected to the souls of human beings in any form such as animal farming (poultry) is not permitted unless it is as a pet not as food. Horses, Donkeys, Dog and other animals that can be trained for a good purpose is permitted, basically, anything that you do not intend to kill are ok. And any other financial business is permitted with truthful accurate dealing, honesty and trust with an agreed percentage of interest and payment period that will be beneficial to each party. Manufacturing of anything that makes life comfortable in a physical way such as cars or provision of electricity, transport etc. are permitted.

All those who do the above positive things are blessed and **THE FATHER** will give them a prosperous life. Police one shall arrest any one who is involved in the above negative forms of business shall be arrested by police one, two and three and they shall be returned to the HOLE and they shall cease to exist.

SPIRITUAL OPERATIONAL PURPOSES- All forms of evil spiritual establishments in the world are not permitted because they not dealing with **THE FATHER, THE CREATOR OF THE UNIVERSE**, they are dealing with elementary spirits. Churches, fraternity of all kinds of a cultism, secret societies, witchcraft, traditional, beating of drums and clapping of hands and orchestral doctrines are not directed by **ME** and not established for **MY** interest. **I** have nothing to do with them. **I** have never, ever, ever established a church and demanded that candle or incense burnt in order to attract **ME** to come to them. What are they doing? Do they suggest that that is **THE FATHER**? They are worshiping elementary spirits or angels and not **ME, THE FATHER GOD, THE CREATOR OF THE UNIVERSE**. **I** have never established anything to initiate in any form. Consider that there is **SOMEONE** who has created this whole world, but you do not hear **HIM** making noises about all these things, do you not fear such a personality? Do you not know who this personality is supposed to be?

Some people establish all these elementary organizations because of money or jealousy. Others establish elementary institutions through being possessed by the planetary spirit that they come from who want to be recognized through them, which **I** call second hand spirits. This is the case of the blind leading the blind.

THE TRUE WORSHIP, THE MODE AND CONDUCT OF WORSHIPING THE FATHER -Wherever you find yourself worship **THE FATHER** there at any point in time. In the air, in the car and even as you are sleeping worship **I THE FATHER, THE CREATOR OF THE UNIVERSE** because **I** lavishly fill the space and **MY** dwelling place is everywhere, here and there. Kneeling down and knocking of your head is to prostrate before **THE FATHER** as the heaven is **MY** throne and the earth is **MY** footstool, and so whenever you kneel down and knock your head and communicate with **ME**, **I** will answer you. The only condition is that you have to purify your heart and forgive one another, and make peace with your adversary, without which you will not see **THE FATHER** and this is the only condition. Do all this through In the Name and Blood our Lord Jesus Christ and all is well.

CONGREGATION- To congregate with one another does not mean worshiping **THE FATHER**. There are two different congregations that exist, congregation of the righteousness and congregation of the unrighteousness. All the children of God from the offspring of human God, the first son of **THE FATHER**, Adam and Eve form the larger congregation of Brotherhood as one flock and one shepherd and that is the congregation of righteousness which means the children of one parent. All those who believe that they came from this family are called into this one movement, The Kingdom of God, brotherhood of the Cross and star.

MODE OF DRESSING- Mode of dressing is the symbol of righteousness and that is the white garment to represent the pure and peaceful co-existing of the children of God.

THE DIRECTION OF SPIRITUAL BENEFIT FROM THE FATHER- All the true children of **THE FATHER** who have one problem or the other, and are weak in spirit, either in the form of sickness or misfortune, should, according to their believe, fast and pray either from six am to twelve pm or six am to six pm or one day dry according to their ability, and **THE FATHER** will take their problem away. If they do this and their problem persists, they should go on ministry work in a spiritual hospital for physical attention. If their problem requires physical attention a charity worker will see to them and through this ministry work they will be well. They should avoid taking part in the traditional methods of doing things in the form of usage of herbs or other mixtures that are not unauthorized by **THE FATHER** then stating **THE FATHER** approves, **I** do not. The approve three items of healing are **The Spoken Word, Holy Oil and Holy**

Water, sanctified and blessed by **THE FATHER** through the minister of faith. Anything more than that is not from **ME**. This shall be operated under charity.

INDIVIDUAL TALENT - Every human being created by **THE FATHER** has one or more talents to benefit themselves and others. These talents form the division of labor in **THE FATHERS** system. Everybody must recognize and respect another person's positive talent and help to promote and develop it, so that they will benefit from each other.

APPRECIATION- From now on till eternity, **I** know and **I** have confirmed that human kind refuses to appreciate the spiritual talents of their brothers and sisters because it is God that does all works and wonders thereby using that to debar those who have spiritual talents so that they are not able to benefit from their talents because it is spiritual in nature.

They make statements such as 'it was done by **THE FATHER'**. Due to the lack of the good gestures in appreciating the spiritual talents of brethren, some people have decided to charge for it, which is not permitted by **ME**, and those who cannot charge have decided to stop the spiritual work because it leaves them poor. For this reason, **I AM** going to correct this situation. **I** decree from this budget that those who do spiritual work should have more things. In fact more than what other people enjoy, because they are spiritual supporter. If any spiritual person attends to you for any service in a positive way as a spiritual witness, even by the power of pronouncement, and you do not show practical appreciation, it will be deducted from your spiritual account to that of the spiritual witness's and in addition to that, the work may not be effective. You should consider supporting the spiritual person more than ten parts from what you earn, because that is work for your soul. And if a spiritual person uses 'corny' (trickery) to take money from people, **I** will take money from their spiritual account with interest for the person they tricked and the spiritual person will also loose his or her talent.

GOVERNMENT WORKERS- Every government worker starting from the highest post, be it Head of States, Prime Ministers Presidents, Kings and Queens, Princes and Princesses, Chairman or Mayor of the local government etc, etc, are the servants for their people. They should be paid enough money that is suitable to their post and they should not embezzle any public funds for any reason, if they do, the angels will arrest them. They should be true children of **THE FATHER** and not belong to any secret society, and should not promote human animal emblems.

SERVANTS- All forms of servants should be honest to their masters and take directives from their masters, if they so wish to work for their master then they should not kick against their master, as that will bring destruction to their soul. And the master should treat the servant well and give them their full entitlement to make them feel like human beings. Any party that does not do likewise will be demoted and there is a consequence for disobeying **THE FATHER'S** instruction.

EMPLOYEES AND EMPLOYERS- If anybody accepts to work for somebody and agrees the payment and later decides that the money is not enough and cannot negotiate more payment, they should not strike because it is evil. If they do not want to stay, they should resign and look for another job. And the employer should honor the terms of employment. And if they want to terminate the employee's employment, they should give the employee enough entitlement and enough time for the employee to seek other employment. Any party that does not do this will be demoted and there is a consequence for disobeying **THE FATHER'S** instruction.

BROTHERS AND SISTERS- every human being on earth are brothers and sisters despite coming from different physical parents, because we are all from one **ALMIGHTY FATHER GOD**. Whether in a family there be different fathers or different mothers, we are all brothers and sisters and should love one another and not practice partiality, with the exception of this order, you will be demoted and there is a consequence for disobeying **THE FATHER'S** instruction.

PARENTS AND CHILDREN- Parents should love and treat their children well, knowing that **THE ALMIGHTY FATHER**, The Creator is their original

FATHER, and they are only caretakers for a short period. The parent should speak the word of blessing to develop the children in the positive way for **THE FATHER**, and they should not expect more than what they themselves are doing or have done for their parents. They should not forget that **I** pay every parent, for having and bringing their children up because their reward is in **MY** hand, and not in the children's hands. So any parent that curses their children will answer to **ME,** because they fight against **ME**, and obstruct **MY** creations. Every parent has the authority to train and control their children for twelve years, after that the child/ren can learn from their parents for six years up till eighteen years, after that they are free to live their lives and no parent should enslave their children. Children should obey their parents only in the positive way of knowing **THE FATHER** and to develop characters that will be beneficial to their life, and that is the commandment for how to live long on earth. Children should appreciate their parents housing them if possible, clothing them if possible, because they first housed them, and clothed them when they were naked and that will bring blessing for them, whether the parent is good or not. Any party that does not do likewise will be demoted and there is a consequence for disobeying **THE FATHER'S** instruction.

HUSBAND AND WIFE-husband and wife should love themselves and treat themselves as one body and one flesh believing that through that they can have good children that will bring a good family, and if it happens that one of the partners makes a mistake and commits adultery, the other who did not commit adultery whose love remains strong agrees that they confess their sins and forgive themselves then they have the right to continue with their marriage. **I THE FATHER** will also forgive them through the blood of Our Lord Jesus The Christ, if the good partner decides not to forgive the one that has made the mistake then they should separate without one trying to destroy one another. **MY** soul will not tolerate any body that tries to condemn or judge another person because of one reason or the other. Everybody shall leave in total freedom, and they shall receive their judgment in due cause, but everyone should live in peace. Any party that does not do likewise will be demoted and there is a consequence for disobeying **THE FATHER'S** instruction.

STUDENT OF ACADEMIA OR APPRENTICE OF TRAINING- All students of any form should be subjected to their masters. Children of God are not permitted to learn anything that will bring discomfort or harm to human being. Both the student and the master are not exempt. The student should not learn any carnal thing and the master should not teach any evil in the name of study or knowledge that is not from **THE FATHER**. If they disobey this instruction they shall be destroyed and returned to the HOLE and they shall cease to exist.

FRIENDS- The reason that leads to two people or more to become friends should be positive not evil and negative. Friends should not betray each other. Any party that does not do likewise will be demoted and there is a consequence for disobeying **THE FATHER'S** instruction.

GOVERNMENT SERVICES AND INDIVIDUAL TAX- Every government that establishes should represent **THE FATHER** should not be partial and suppress people and every government should recognize **THE FATHER, THE CREATOR OF THE UNIVERSE**. Every government should provide free roads, free water, and free systems of communication such as telephone, and free electricity or gas. Then the citizen should pay one common tax to cover the bills. For instance in a year, they should pay 100 pounds that should be deducted directly from their salary. There should be a national charity for every one that is unemployed, disabled, and pensioners and all those in need should be taken care of, from children to adults, men and women. Governments should not spend God's money in going to war or buy weapons rather, they should use the money to look after the whole world for every one to live comfortably and they should train people free up till basic educational level such as secondary school. The government should pay all ministers of God and as a first priority; there should be a ministries for God's affairs and messengers.

THIS IS THE BUDGET I HAVE MADE TODAY-
I have blessed the entire world, all children of God. This is the budget I have

made today on the 0A of Peter, BOOD (first April 04) spiritually to be activated physically on the OA Peter BOOG (first April 07). Those who hearken and believe any of **MY** instruction are blessed spiritually and physically and otherwise. Those who disobey shall face the consequence and they will be returned to the HOLE and they will cease to exist. **I** know that it is only the human animals that are going to disobey; children of God have no problem.

Let **MY** peace and blessing abide with the entire world.
Now and forever more Amen.

THE SOUL WORLD OF ABC OF WORD

The Three Worlds of the Word

A. The Spiritual world of the WORD is the Thought

B. The Soul world of the WORD is the Speech.

C. The Physical world of the WORD is Physical print of the word e.g.: WRITING (what the eye can behold) the completion: SPIRIT, SOUL AND BODY.

> *Song:*
> *__HE__ is the quickening spirit, he's the quickening spirit, __HE__ moves around the universe, he is the quickening spirit*
>
> *Song:*
> *In the beginning was the word and the word was God. In the beginning was the word and the word was God*

THE REVELATION OF THE FATHER GOD THE KING OF KINGS AND THE LORD OF LORDS TO KING SOLOMON DAVID JESSE ETE

The *Spiritual* world of the word is **THE FATHER GOD ALMIGHTY, HE IS THE FATHER, THE CREATOR OF THE UNIVERSE LEADER OLUMBA OLUMBA OBU THE LAST TOTAL WORD PERSONIFIED HOLY SPIRIT OF TRUTH,** The Sole Spiritual Head of the Universe, The office of the proprietorship the owner, to direct and to own.

The *Soul world* of the word is **The King of Kings and Lord of Lords,** Adam. **(HIS HOLINESS OLUMBA OLUMBA OBU "THE UNIVERSAL SHRINE" OF THE SUPREME WORD)** representing the spoken word or speech, The Christhood office and the Kingship title to manage the **FATHER'S** affairs or **FATHER'S** business.

The *Physical True World* of the Word is the *Physical Servant* in the world for the word is **Abel,** (King Solomon David Jesse ETE), representing the servant ship office, the house of the positive word, (FATHER'S TALK (GOD PRESENT) KING SOLOMON SPIRITUAL LIBRARY the promoter of the WORD and to carry out the instruction of the word. This is the Physical HARDWARE for the WORD.

THE ABOVE IS THE COMPLETION OF THE ABC OF THE WORD AND THE POWER!
Enye, Odudu Abasi Me, OOO, Zim Zim Zim, Asaso

When the *Word* is silent in the heart, it is the **THOUGHT** (THE HOLY FATHER). **HE** is the spirit WORD.

When the *Word* is spoken through the tongue, the hyphen of the mouth, **HE** is the **WORD** (THE HOLY SON OF THE FATHER), which represents the inner soul of The Father God, the total energy of God; the **SOUL** world of the **WORD** to manifest all objects souls of creations.

When the order of the *Word* is carried out practically, that is the manifestation of the word representing the **PHYSICAL** world of the **WORD.** For this reason, the manifestation is the *'Servant-ship office'* to put the word into action to bring the *Word* into physical reality. The office of **THE FATHER** is one. The office of the son-ship is one and the office of the servant ship belongs to every positives creation, the sons and the daughters of God, the positive humans

SPIANZATICE AMANTICE- postpone the word for now or hold on, *(This is when The Father postponed the revelation due to persistent noise).*

Song:
I have come, I have come
I have come to change the world
I have come, I have come, I have come to change the world

SPADIANTICE-AMANTICE- release the word now *(This is when **THE FATHER** brought back the word)*

Song:
*Everything is good because **THE FATHER** make it so; everything is well everything is well because **THE FATHER** makes it so.*

I AM revealing this revelation, because of the attitude of human beings, especially the children of disobedience, whose duty is always to ignore, to obstruct, to barrier and to fight against the will of **THE FATHER GOD**. I have decided to reveal most of the hidden secrets through this medium called '**FATHER TALK AS MY PRESENT**' via the Senior Christ Servant King Solomon David Etteh (**MY** cold brain, meaning **THE FATHER'S** inner bedroom) in world of the word, **I AM every where, here and there** and I talk through everybody just as **I AM** talking through the Senior Christ Servant King Solomon David Etteh not because King Solomon Etteh is good or bad, than anybody else in this world, but because everybody has their assignment and their purpose of being created by **THE FATHER**. From the beginning of time **I** made King Solomon for this purpose. King Solomon means a cold store room, a storage, which is unlimited in capacity; **HE** is a cold brain, which means 'peace of The Father' (Solomon ETE). Cold brain means wisdom **UNLIMITED**

MEMORIES, and the storage or storekeeper means servant. That was Abel, the positive son of Adam, the second thought of **THE FATHER GOD**, the spiritual house, the first soul in the world of incarnation. That is why anybody that is jealous of somebody and hates somebody destroys himself or herself unknowingly, because you do not know who somebody is and your spiritual link to that person and you do not even know who you yourself are. Everything seen and unseen comes out from **ME THE FATHER GOD. FATHER** means one thing which cannot be divided, there is no second and no deputy, **there is nothing like THE FATHER except THE FATHER and everything comes out from THE FATHER** and when it manifest, first into the Spirit object or a formula object (the spiritual form) next to the Soul object and from there it manifest physically in the true form, therefore, **THE FATHER** is one, then projected

HIMSELF into many things called the shadow of object. The shadow of object can also project itself into the physical object, but shadow of object is one that produces an object physically then the physical object can be used as a material to pre-plant the multiple objects for multiple souls by **THE FATHER HIMSELF**. **THE FATHER** can create together with **HIS** soul, the Spoken Word, **THE FATHER'S** son, the total energy of **THE FATHER GOD**. And the soul can only be created through word in man. For this reason, **FATHER**, the Word and the man is one entity -Trinity in heaven and trinity on earth. That is God's present is equal to one. **IWEUS**, With this understanding, **I** hope that *all senior citizens of the new Age* will never be jealous when **THE FATHER** is using somebody to do one thing or the other in the positive way. The carnal children of this world are mistaken and quote themselves wrongly by saying that God is a jealous God. Today, before **I** proceed further, **I** have to defend **MYSELF** against the incorrect concept that suggests that God is a jealous God. Which God? **I** hope that it is not **THE FATHER GOD?** Because it is wrong, **I AM** not a jealous **FATHER**. Jealousy is evil; it is the senior spirit of Satan. Anybody that has jealousy can never do anything good that benefits another person, a jealous heart blocks the way against LOVE, the spirit of God.

Nothing good can come out of the heart of jealousy. When you are jealous, you are in darkness and you are blind and all doors of goodness are closed against you and you remain in total darkness. From there the jealous mind projects all manner of evil around him. The first one is hatred, telling lies against the one you are jealous of. Partiality, hypocrisy and envy, all lead to killing. Therefore when people say that **THE FATHER** is a jealous **FATHER** do **ME, THE FATHER GOD** do all these things mentioned above? If **THE FATHER GOD** is a jealous God would **HE** have created man and called him **MY** beloved son? If Christ was jealous, would He have died for man? So, **THE FATHER GOD** is not a jealous **FATHER**. **I** repeat, whoever that is jealous in the evil way against somebody will never progress in the soul and will be returned to the HOLE and they will cease to exist.

I AM only interested about **MY** spirit in you and that brings you salvation, because **I** will not see you perish, that, is the meaning of **THE FATHER** being jealous. So **I AM** defending **MYSELF** through this revelation. His Holiness, The King of Kings and The Lord of Lords Olumba Olumba Obu and **MY** Senior Servant, King Solomon David Etteh THE ABEL - LIVE SOUL WORD'S SERVANT and all positive children of **THE FATHER**

are not jealous. What belongs to **THE FATHER** belongs to them. We are one.

THANK YOU FATHER

Copyright © 2004 Kssl/hrmkingsdetteh All Rights Reserved

KING SOLOMON SPIRITUAL LIBRARY

THE GOD ENCYCLOPAEDIA WORD OF INFINITY

==========

King Solomon Spiritual Library,
God Universal Information Centre
Father's Talk (God Present)

WITH LOVE

Covered: This **BOOK,** e-book, software or software's, books, website, video, audio, idea or ideas, formula or formulas, manual or instruction manual.

... Hereby gives you a non-exclusive license to use the ... (THIS BOOK).
Some of the word here is coded with the (WORD OF SUPER HOLY AND INTELLIGENCE FATHER GOD ALMIGHTY)

Title, ownership rights, and intellectual property rights in and to the Website, Books, E-book, Audios and Videos, Shops and Store – e-Stores, Fundraisings, Celebrations and the supreme word seasons Celebration formulas and arrangement, Positive Inspiration, Holy (Fata), FATHER GOD ALMIGHTY POSSESSING SPIRIT in thought, in words and in did, thinking well, speaking well, hearing well and doing well shall remain in me and in ... The BOOK is protected by international copyright.

FATHER'S TALK (GOD PRESENT)

The message in The Father's Talk (GOD PRESENT) does not challenge any authority either individuals, groups or governments of any land or even any belief of any form. It is rather challenging the truth that is hidden from mankind. Therefore, any spirit, soul or physical human being who decides to challenge this truth shall have himself or herself to blame.

Key A

Any individual that reads any of The Father's Talk (GOD PRESENT) with faith; love and acceptance will experience immediate positive change in his or her life from spirit, soul to physical. If he or she accepts the message then he or she will be free from any evil.

Key B: **PEACE AND LOVE**
If you do not believe the contents of any of The Father's Talk (GOD PRESENT) it is possible through The Father's divine love and peace simply hands over your copy to a friend or somebody else that would like to keep a copy, or signing out from any of the website that connected to The Father's Talk (GOD PRESENT) KING SOLOMON SPIRITUAL e-LIBRARY without any evil and negative comments and you are blessed and free.

========

FROM THE DESK OF INSPIRATIONAL HEAD

Fees, Prices and Donations; There is no refund on fees, price or donations since your fees price or donations are using as a charity contribution to do administration work of THE SUPREME WORD, So please kindly read this first before you decide to involves yourself in any of the under mention of HRM King Solomon David Jesse ETE universal Inspirational Businesses of (GOD PRESENT) in cash, kinds and otherwise.

I CAME FROM THE FATHER GOD, WITH THE FATHER GOD, AND BY THE FATHER GOD TO ESTABLISH THE FOLLOWING:

Therefore, all distributors and contributors of The Father's Talk (GOD PRESENT), The Spiritual Advice, Healing and Counselling on General Live (The Universal

Supreme Spiritual General Hospital), New Songs and Psalms of King David and Solomon, The Word of **GOD** Processing City in Ikot Okwo or e-City online, The Trinity Celebration, **"OUC FUND"**, The Universal Bank Account For All Creations, **"ERUFA"** ETE Royal Universal Family, **"THEUNISAL-SUREME SEACELION"** The Universal Supreme Word Season Celebration To Appreciates THE FATHER GOD ALMIGHTY **"THEUNI-SUREME WORA THECRO-THEUNISE" The Universal Supreme Word Almighty, THE CREATOR OF THE UNIVERSE** should attach this information to all readers, website visitors, distributors, affiliates person/group, celebrant and celebrations centres, supporters and promoters, members, workers and voluntary workers, Ete royal universal palace committee, governments and many other centres as an agreement. Please kindly know that I am not answering to any physical human except **PEACE, UNITY AND LOVE.**

"**THEUNISAL-SUREME WORA THECRO-THEUNISE**".

I AM IN THE STAGE OF SUPER HOLY AND INTELLIGENCE FATHER GOD POSITIVE MADNESS OF THE HOLY SPIRIT OF TRUTH, ENYEN ODUDU ODUDU ODUDU ABASI MI OOO ZIM ZIM ZIM ASSASU, POSITIVE POSITIVE POSITIVE. UKEMEKE AKA IDIOK UNAM.

Let the peace and blessing of the Holy Father abide with everybody who corporate with this divine Father's Talk (GOD PRESENT

THANK YOU FATHER
BY
THE HOLY SPIRIT OF THE FATHER GOD
THROUGH HIS SERVANT
Senior Christ Servant
HRM King Solomon David Jesse ETE
Brotherhood of the
Cross and STAR
Eteroyal Universal family
Ikot Okwo The Great City of Refuge, Ete Community
Ikot Abasi LGA-543001
Akwa Ibom State Nigeria-W/A
Tel. 0803663841
Email: ksslibrary@eteroyalmail.com

www.ingramcontent.com/pod-product-compliance
Lightning Source LLC
Chambersburg PA
CBHW021835220426
43663CB00005B/256